PHILLIPA MITCHELL

FOUR IN·THE MORNING

BASED ON A TRUE STORY

First published in 2023 by Phillipa Mitchell

Content © Phillipa Mitchell

www.phillipamitchell.com

Paperback ISBN 978-0-7961-3424-0

Also available as an e-book

Front cover design by Gregg Davies Media

www.greggdavies.com

Printed in the United States of America

All rights reserved

The moral right of the author has been asserted.

No part of this publication may be reproduced, distributed, or transmitted in any form or by any means, including photocopying, recording, or other electronic or mechanical methods, without the prior written permission of the author, except in the case of brief quotations embodied in critical reviews and certain other non-commercial uses permitted by copyright law.

Contents

Dedication	VI
CHAPTER 1	1
CHAPTER 2	18
CHAPTER 3	64
CHAPTER 4	80
CHAPTER 5	94
CHAPTER 6	109
CHAPTER 7	125
CHAPTER 8	137
CHAPTER 9	161

CHAPTER 10	177
CHAPTER 11	189
CHAPTER 12	202
CHAPTER 13	215
CHAPTER 14	236
CHAPTER 15	257
CHAPTER 16	271
CHAPTER 17	295
CHAPTER 18	315
CHAPTER 19	329
CHAPTER 20	356
CHAPTER 21	385
CHAPTER 22	410
CHAPTER 23	430

Epilogue	441
Acknowledgements	448
About the Author	451
Chapter	453

This book is dedicated to Grant. Because you will always be loved, and you will never be forgotten.

CHAPTER 1

She woke from her sleep with her heart pounding in her chest and her eyes darting wildly around the room. She could still hear his voice in her head.

"I'll never take you back!" he hissed down the phone. "I'll never take you back."

A click. And then silence.

This was the last time they would speak.

A few weeks earlier

Were we once?

She let her eyes take in the words as she felt a tremble down her spine and her heart skip a beat. It had been seventeen years. She was a grown woman, married with two children. She was running a successful business, living in a beautiful home and, to the outside world, she had the perfect life.

Not knowing what the message itself contained, she slowly pointed her mouse over the words, clicked, and held her breath.

Hi Claudia! Are you currently married? I am trying to remember your maiden name. Do you, by any chance, remember me? Regards, Alex

A year earlier

Sometimes, in the depths of one's despair, a knight in shining armour comes along, sweeps us up off the dusty earth, and carries us away from the life we were desperate to leave behind. Over a period of time, grateful for being rescued and unsure of the place to which this all might lead, a person may become shrouded with feelings of guilt in return for the kindness that was shown, the reasons for which will be explained shortly.

Loneliness and lovelessness is a terrible place to be. Claudia and Gareth had been married for twelve rather platonic years. He never ceased reminding her of how he had been there for her all those years ago and that if it were not for him and his family, she would have never amounted to much. Claudia truly believed that he was right and always acknowledged the debt that she owed him, even though she did not know how she was ever going to be able to repay him. As the years melted away, she struggled to love him. She wondered sometimes whether she had ever really been in love with him or whether the love that existed between them was more obligatory from her side. Love on extended credit terms, as if he'd been a love loan shark of sorts.

He was depressed and took a sadistic pleasure in bringing her bright soul down with him. His scathing tongue and judgemental nature often left her reeling. Her soul shrank as he demeaned her and criticised her in front of his family and her friends. How could a man who professed to love her so much speak to her as if she meant nothing to him? She would watch movies where two people would connect on such a deep level that they were virtually inseparable. She watched as couples would hug each other and kiss each other, not out of any form of marital obligation but from a place of absolute love. Sadly, Claudia realised that what she had with Gareth was not love, and yet she longed to experience this with every fibre of her being.

Eighteen months earlier

The human spirit is a funny thing. When it feels undernourished, it eventually tires of the depravity and goes off in search of sustenance. Sometimes, it is actively sought out; other times, it invites itself in unannounced.

A deep friendship had formed between the two women, both of whom were unconsciously seeking a way out of the mundaneness of their loveless marriages. It began with their two young children, who had formed a bond at school, culminating in numerous social invitations, which often continued late into the evenings.

Their time spent together was often one of each woman unburdening her soul, each seeking a deeper meaning in their stories. Denise had been repeatedly molested by her stepfather as a young girl, and he was serving time in prison for murdering her mother in cold blood. He had walked in on Denise's mother and a lover briefly after their separation and, in a blinding rage, had returned to his car to retrieve his pistol and turned it on both of them. Denise's mother was wrenched from her life, and she was left to put the shattered pieces of her life back together.

The deep friendship soon became more than that. The two women felt as if their souls were intertwined, and each began experiencing feelings towards the other that went far beyond the boundaries of friendship.

It was New Year's Eve. Denise, her husband and their children were spending the night at Claudia and Gareth's holiday home at a dam out in the countryside. The revelry continued late into the night as the house party became a street party, and copious amounts of intoxicating liquids were consumed.

Gareth had left the party and was spying on a set of neighbours who were performing carnal acts behind semi-closed curtains. Denise and Claudia had, with their arms around each other's waists, teetered up the street, holding each other up, giggling uncontrollably. Denise's husband had passed out in one of the outside chairs, and they quietly crept past him. Closing the door, they both fell on to the bed in the master suite, whispering and reminiscing about the evening's events. The chatter soon quietened, and the two women found themselves locked in each other's embrace. They stared into each other's eyes, both knowing that they were on the brink of crossing into forbidden territory, while the fuzziness of inebriation removed the usual boundaries of inhibition.

Breathing quickened, and hands snaked around the other's body, each craving the contact of the other one's skin. Lips parted and touched, and soon, the two women were completely lost in each other, each feeling the relief of the longing that they had both kept at arm's length from each other for what seemed like an excruciating amount of time.

Suddenly, the bedroom door swung open and glaring at the two women from the shadows stood Gareth, his eyes wild with hurt and anger.

"I knew it," he seethed. "I knew that there was something going on between the two of you!"

The words shot through Claudia's heart, and suddenly, a deep sense of sobriety came over her. Denise hurriedly straightened her clothes and stumbled off the bed, apologising as she pushed past Gareth in the doorway.

"It's not what you think, Gareth," Claudia pleaded, suddenly realising what it must have looked like through her husband's eyes and feeling secretly relieved that it had not gone any further than it did. With tears running uncontrollably down her face and mascara streaking across her cheekbones, wishing the world would swallow her up, she reeled as Gareth yelled at her to leave the room. Claudia stood in the passageway, feeling the floors and the walls vibrate as he slammed the bedroom door behind her. It was then that she knew that her life had changed its course and that when the sun rose, friendships would need to be reassessed, and a marriage would need to be rebuilt.

Yet when the sun's golden fingers reached through the gaps in the curtains and played with the curls of hair that fell across her face, Claudia awoke, not with a gripping sense of fear in her heart, but rather a sense of peace. Peace at having opened her soul up to another human being, someone who loved her unconditionally, someone who *got* her, someone who made her feel that she was *worthy* and not some dismal failure with an almost suffocating debt that hung over her head like a sword.

She rose from the sofa and slowly tiptoed towards the bedroom where Denise and her husband were still fast asleep, Denise's husband oblivious to what had happened within metres of where he had been sleeping the previous evening. She looked down at her friend, wondering how she would feel when she awoke and how they would plan their way forward, each knowing that so much had been said and yet so much had been left unsaid while an even deeper connection had been forged between the two women.

Claudia walked over to the master bedroom, the door still shut. She grasped the cold metal handle and turned it. It clicked, but the door was locked. She suddenly felt the fear welling up from her stomach and wrapping its icy fingers around her throat. She felt as if she was a prisoner, a trespasser, even though she was on the other side of the cell. Breathing in slowly through her teeth and feeling the skin on her neck prickle with dread and trepidation, she made a fist and quietly knocked on the door.

"Gareth," she whispered. "Gareth, are you awake? Please open the door."

At first, there was silence, but then she heard movement behind the door and then the key turning in the lock. The door slowly opened, and Gareth stood there, staring at her with a look of disappointment and disbelief in his eyes.

"I don't know what you want me to say to you," he said quietly under his breath. "I don't know what to say."

Claudia felt the tears welling up in her eyes as she realised the enormity of what he had witnessed the night before.

"Can I come in? Can we just talk this through? I need you to hear me out," she whispered, worried about waking Denise and her husband in the room next door.

Gareth stepped back to allow Claudia to walk past him. She sat down on the edge of the bed, her face cupped in her hands.

"We were drunk," she said as he stood against the closed door, looking down at her. "I don't even know how it happened – it all happened so fast. I thought we were going to lie down and pass out after everything we'd had to drink. I didn't know where you were. I wasn't even thinking about you because I knew you'd probably gone and joined another party."

"What the hell were you thinking?" he whispered loudly. "We're married, and we have two children – are you ready to just throw everything away? For her? What about us?"

Claudia sat staring blankly at the floor, her body completely numb, thoughts rushing through her head but being unable to hold on to even just one of them.

"Gareth, there's no love left between us," she whispered, her voice trembling. "Even though I am still coming to terms with what happened last night, I know that none of this would have happened if we'd just worked through our stuff when we had the chance. I love you, but I'm no longer *in love* with you. You can't give me the love that I need, but I've found that love in Denise. I love her so much, so much that my heart aches. And yet, I have such a deep sense of responsibility towards you and the boys. I can't let our marriage go, but I can't let her go either. I just need some time to work things out. I know I've hurt you, and I know it's going to take time for you to forgive me, but I feel as if we've reached a turning point in our marriage, and we've got to figure out how we can fix this – *if* we can even begin to fix this."

Gareth slumped against the wall and sighed.

"Okay," he said. "I really love you, and I don't want to lose you, but I am confused, and I don't know how to make room for a third person in our relationship. Does Denise feel the same? What about her kids and her marriage?"

"I don't know," Claudia said, wiping the tears away from her eyes. "Everything just seems so complicated. We haven't spoken since last night, so I don't even know what she's thinking or feeling or whether she even remembers what happened."

Gareth straightened his body against the wall and opened the bedroom door. "Look, I really don't know what to do right now. Let's just try to get through the day. We can try to work this out once they're gone. I'm going to make coffee."

He turned and left the room, and Claudia lifted her head and stared at herself in the dressing table mirror. Twenty-four hours ago, everything had been so different.

"Morning!" she heard Denise's voice calling through the doorway. "You sleep well, my friend?"

Claudia looked up at Denise and smiled. "Yeah, and you?"

Denise laughed and went on to explain in great detail that their bed had been attacked by an army of ants and that she thought they had carried her out of the bed during the night.

"How are you feeling after last night?" Claudia asked, desperately trying to figure out whether last night had even happened in her friend's eyes.

"Oh, a bit of a headache, but I'll be okay," she smiled. "Where's Gareth?"

"Making coffee," said Claudia, "He's in a bit of a bad space this morning, so just be careful when you go through, okay?"

Denise's eyes widened, and then she smiled. "Don't worry, I'll go and talk to him. Everything will be alright."

Claudia suddenly felt empty. How was it possible that something that had meant everything to her had meant so little to Denise? She was practically skirting around the subject as if nothing had happened. Confused and sad, she got up and took a long shower, letting the water wash away her hopes and fantasies and dreams of happiness. She felt like a complete idiot.

Sometimes, the Universe plays tricks on us – mind games designed to make us reassess our perceived realities. Sometimes those tricks are unfair and taunting, like bullies on a playground, spinning around like a merry-go-round, chasing and teasing and cruelly laughing; and sometimes they are like rose-tinted lenses, making things appear to be in a state of blissful perfection for a period of time, only to be shattered by a word, or a look, or a thought, or a deed.

In Claudia's case, it was the sight of Denise's car driving off down the road later that day, windows open and children's hands waving out the back windows. A feeling of emptiness crept into her soul like a thick cloud of fog over a dusty township on a winter's morning.

༄

After a few days of stilted conversation, Claudia decided that she could no longer stand the gaping cavern that had opened up between her and Denise. She picked up the telephone and asked that they meet – sooner rather than later.

It was a wintery day, but they sat outside under the weak rays of winter sunlight. Finally, Claudia could say everything she'd been holding on to.

"Denise," she started, biting her lower lip nervously. "How much of what happened on New Year's Eve do you remember? I'm not talking about the party, though – I'm talking about what happened between you and me when Gareth walked in on us."

Denise sighed and crossed her arms.

"Look, Claudia," she said uneasily. "I remember what happened. It's a bit hazy, but I remember enough. I love you, my friend, so much, but we've got to pretend this never happened. I can't wreck the life I've worked so hard to build for my family just for the sake of my own selfish needs. God, I would do anything for it to just be the two of us together. We understand each other. We're soul mates. I've never connected with anyone like I've connected with you. But no, this chapter needs to be closed. It never happened, okay?"

It was with those words that Claudia's world shattered and tinkled to the floor in a million little pieces. She felt a gust of wind blowing around her feet and watched the pieces drift off into the sky like tiny dandelions, and she knew in that moment that she had no choice but to bring her focus back to Gareth and find a way, any possible way, to dig deep into her heart and soul and reconnect with her husband. It was either that, or she was going to have to make her own way in the world, just her and the children. She had always said that she'd rather be alone and happy than in a relationship where she'd lost all sense of who she was and where she was going. And in truth, it was the latter rather than the former that rang true for her right then.

CHAPTER 2

Seventeen Years Earlier

The great enigma of life is its circle of often unintended beginnings and incongruent endings that, over time, loop around into new and yet completely unforeseen beginnings and endings. Circumstances that flow backwards and forwards like waves in the ocean, sometimes gentle and serene but other times tumultuous and unsettling as they crash into the shoreline like an angry fist pummels a table.

Occasionally a restless and impatient current will pull you backwards away from safety, sucking you into a dark abyss of swirling water while you scramble for safety as sharp rocks and seaweed pull away from under your desperate grip as you are washed further and further away from the shore.

Claudia found herself walking into the sea of her life, scrunching the sand under her toes and allowing the gentle tide to pull the straws of sand out from under her feet.

For seventeen years, Claudia's diary had remained tucked away in the back of a cupboard like a time capsule waiting to be reopened. It was her diary from her final year of school, a time when she had documented a period in her life when she had met a shy young man with stars in his eyes who captured her heart and her soul and sent her on an emotional rollercoaster of undiscovered truths and painful reckonings.

The relationship ended as quickly as it had begun as Claudia walked away from Alex with a chasmal hole in her heart. Their lives had been crushed by the merciless hand of Fate, who had decided that the timing for their souls to be together hadn't been quite right.

But a new script was being written to bring them together again.

As one year flowed into another, Claudia would often come across her diary and secretly open it up to travel back in time. She would find herself catching her breath as she saw his name written in her handwriting on those yellowing pages. How she longed to see him again…

Claudia's sister Elizabeth – who was eleven years younger than her – had been begging Claudia to sign up for the 2007's latest craze: Facebook.

Claudia was in her early thirties, and even though she was proud of being an "early adopter", she really didn't see what all the fuss was about, thinking that it was more of a social spot for teens than a hangout for old friends and lovers, and had put off signing up for some time.

Eventually, however, she conceded to the relentless demands of her over-enthusiastic sister, and before she knew it, she had her own profile and was signing up to interest groups and hunting down old friends.

She joined the group for her high school, wondered for a moment whether Alex had perhaps signed up, searched for a few minutes, found nothing, and moved on.

She didn't think for one second that he'd been searching for her for all this time until one day, out of the blue, she read his message in her Inbox.

It was a message she had been waiting half her life for.

It began with the words, *"Were we once?..."*

Her heart was pounding in her chest. Her pulse was racing, her inner tide was rising, and she wasn't sure whether she should swim for shore or let it take her out to sea. Her fingers trembled above the keyboard. She held her breath as she clicked through to his profile.

And there he was. Her boy. Her childhood sweetheart. How had she missed him when she searched for him before? Oh, it was his middle name, she realised; he had used his full name on his profile.

Alex Rhys Winterton

She took his name in, one word at a time.

She scoured his profile for clues about his life. Was he married? Did he have children? Where in the world had he ended up?

She went back to his message.

Reply. Click.

She started typing…

29 July, 9:45 am

Claudia Stevenson

Alex, of course, I remember you! It feels so surreal typing to you right now after all these years.

Yes, I am married, as I see you are, too. I've been married to Gareth for twelve years now, and we share two children, both boys. Ross is six years old, and Kyle is eleven.

It really is amazing reconnecting with you again. I've often wondered how you are and what you have been up to. I would love to hear more about your life since we left off, so please write back soon.

She closed her eyes and submitted her reply, wondering if and when he would write again.

Every day, she checked her inbox, but each one yielded the same result: nothing.

Hours became days, days drifted into weeks, and then, one day, there was a message...

11 August, 22:52 pm

Alex Winterton

Hi Claudia,

I am so glad to have made contact with you! It has been far too many years, and so many memories have come rushing back to me.

As for the wondering, I've pretty much done the same over the years.

I am married – correct – to Christine, and have been now for nearly six years. No children of our own yet – we are just focusing on our various businesses and passions.

And you? I assume life treats you well and that you have all the things you have desired for yourself?

I am really looking forward to hearing more from you.

A temporary cheers for now...

Claudia's excitement at her reconnection with Alex was palpably absurd, but at the same time, it felt so damn right. She found herself questioning her life and her happiness while Alex consumed more and more of her thoughts.

Since her relationship with Denise, Claudia had promised Gareth that she would never keep anything from him again or allow anything to threaten their marriage. She had been working hard to put the pieces back together again, but she often felt that all she had been left with was shards and splinters of a life that was trapped in a perfect storm.

And now there was Alex.

She felt responsible for the breakdown in her marriage, and Gareth continued to remind her of her innocent infidelity.

How she wished she could find that same love that she had experienced with Denise with her husband. But his scathing tongue continued to push her further away from him, and Claudia started to feel herself being pulled into the swell of the possibility of a rekindled love from nearly two decades before.

Claudia had to force herself from digressing into an unrealistic world of fantasy and romance and deposit herself back on the shore of her life.

But there was someone awaiting a reply from her. There was a lifetime of catching up to do. There was so much that she wanted to say. So much that she needed to say.

12 August, 7:47 am

Claudia Stevenson

I am really thrilled to have reconnected with you again, Alex.

So, where did you and Christine meet up? Anyone I know?

Gareth and I met when I was nineteen. I was going through a rough time at home, and I ended up leaving and moving in with him a few months later. We tied the proverbial knot after four years, and Kyle was born a year later.

I started my own business shortly after that, and Ross was born two years later. Looking back, although it was hectic at the time – building a business and starting a family – it has been so worth the sacrifice. You obviously know what I mean, running your own businesses too. Now, I'm just trying to get more balance in my life.

We bought a holiday house out at a dam in the countryside two years ago (just after my mom passed away – not sure if I ever told you about her and her illness), when I realised life was too short to spend working twenty-four seven. We then decided that this was the lifestyle we wanted permanently, so we put our house on the market, and we're going to be building our dream home in the same estate just as soon as our house sells. I'm visualising starting our new life, and I am sure it will happen before the end of this year.

Do I have all the things I desire for myself? Well, not just yet. Getting there slowly, I guess, one step at a time! And you?

I still can't believe that I am typing to you. You won't believe how many times I've thought about you over the years. It's such a pity we lost touch!

Remember all the fun we had together? Remember our first date at the ice rink where you had to hold me up the whole way around? I'll never forget that night at your place when your mom walked in on us; even though we were fully clothed and behaving ourselves as much as two teenagers under their parents' roof could, I nearly died of embarrassment!

By the way, how are your parents?

I cannot wait to hear from you. Please don't keep me waiting so long this time.

Claudia sat at her desk and smiled to herself. He sounded so different. So mature. In a strange way, their individual commitments to other people and the distance afforded by this digital interface offered a measure of safety where each could explore the other's world without any fear of trespassing into forbidden territory.

The following morning, Claudia found a new message waiting for her from Alex in her inbox.

12 August, 23:43 pm

Alex Winterton

Hi again,

The memories are coming back to me hard and fast. I pretty much remember all our dates. Speaking of which, do you know how difficult it was for me to ask you out on a date the first time?

I remember the walks we used to take from my place to the mall down the road; the ice-skating (or attempts there at) grin...

My ice-skating skills have deteriorated over the years, especially at the thought of landing face-first – or on my butt.

As for getting caught by my mom, I don't think I could ever forget... but then again, you and I had a particular knack for getting caught. If you don't remember the two other occasions, let me remind you: One was at our favourite place: the rooftop of the mall – by a security guard (oh, how I know you must be blushing by now), and the other was at a party in the bathroom with the lights off almost having the door banged down by somebody on the other side (at this stage you should be red in the face – grin.)

I remember our recess breaks at school, where we sat and chatted, and I was always too shy to eat my lunch in your presence. I remember our favourite meeting spot, where you always waited for me on the walkway. I remember how my heart would skip a bit every time I saw you standing there.

I must apologise for taking so long to reply to you the first time. I don't go on to Facebook very often – however, that has changed – I have a real reason to log on now.

I'm really sorry to hear about your mom. What was wrong with her? You never spoke about her.

My parents separated many years ago, and my dad and I, well, we don't talk. In fact, I haven't seen him since the day I came out of the army fifteen years ago. We had a terrible fallout – a rather sad one that.

Did you meet Gareth while you were studying at university?

Christine and I met at a New Year's function in 1998. It was through mutual friends. We have been together ever since, and I proposed to her in Tel Aviv on my birthday six years ago.

Your new home and your new life sound really awesome. Keep up with the visualising; it is the only way to succeed in life and achieve what you really want.

As for desires, well, I guess that's what keeps driving us, hey? I think I, too, am slowly getting there. I have a lot of ambitious goals at the moment. It could be an age thing, but I am looking for quality in everything I do of late.

So, how is all of that for a catch-up? And I didn't even keep you holding on for it. There's a lot more that I would love to hear from you.

Okay, so tag, you're it! I cannot wait.

Claudia was surprised at how much Alex remembered. All this time, she had never realised that she had been as important in his life as he had been in hers. When they broke up, Alex had walked away and continued with his life as if there had never been anything between them, and even though it had been Claudia who initiated the breakup, she was the one who was left with the broken heart.

Reading Alex's words left her with a lump in her throat and a longing to hear more of his memories. Memories that, to Claudia, were a reassurance that not all had been lost.

Gareth was oblivious to the shift in Claudia's world, and Claudia's heart ached, knowing that she was once again treading on forbidden ground. She had wandered too far down this path, and she was being drawn into the light like a moth to a flame. She could not turn herself around and walk back to where she had started out.

13 August, 21:05 pm

Claudia Stevenson

Wow, what memories... Going red with embarrassment, let's try crimson!

There was so much chemistry between the two of us, Alex. I have always said that one of my big regrets with you was that things never went further between us – if you know what I mean. I just had some stupid issues that I was dealing with at the time.

Wow, I've waited a long time to tell you that!

Even though it's seventeen years later, Alex, I have never forgotten you. You were a very special part of my life, my soul mate, and it took me a very, very long time to get over you.

I'll always remember that last Christmas party at the clothing store where we worked together over the weekends. We were all dancing (you were dating someone else then – I think you were engaged to her, actually), and the song "Sacrifice" by Elton John came on, and one of our workmates pushed you and me together on the dance floor. We both felt so awkward, but you put your arms around me and pulled me close to you, and we danced to the rhythm of the music. I felt electrified as your skin touched mine, and I felt your soft breath on my forehead. It was the saddest dance of my life.

When the song ended, we both looked into each other's eyes, not wanting to separate our grasp, but then we did, you turned and walked away and didn't look back. I felt as if I'd sacrificed my soul to the devil – I wanted you back so much. So, needless to say, every time I hear that song, I think of that dance, and you, and everything we lost.

I don't think I ever told you about my mom. She died of Huntington's Disease, a genetic disease that she inherited from her mother. It slowly destroys the person's mind and body, eating away at it until there is nothing left.

I lost touch with her for many years and then discovered her living in a hellhole in a dingy part of town, being beaten daily by a man she'd befriended. He sold all her precious possessions – her books, her furniture, everything he could lay his hands on, to buy booze and feed his drug addiction.

She was living off the kindness of the Salvation Army, who brought food to her every day, and he sold that too.

I eventually called the social workers in, and she was committed to a mental asylum, later moving to a sanatorium where she lived out her days in their Frail Care section. There wasn't really anything that anybody could do for her other than *make her comfortable. She was there for about four years before she died.*

I visited her shortly before she passed away, and she was lying in a child's cot, a shrivelled-up remnant of a once beautiful woman, shouting and screaming at people who weren't even there. She was trapped in schizophrenia, and her lucid moments were few and far between. It was terribly sad.

Yes, I remember your dad. I always liked him. I'm so sorry you had a fallout. What happened? And how is your mom? You didn't mention her?

My dad and I didn't speak for about four years after I left home. I got myself a part-time job and moved in with Gareth. I only started speaking to my parents when Kyle was born; it was quite weird how he brought us all together.

I think it's time for me to sign off now. Gareth is going to start wondering why I'm still in the office, and the last thing I need is for him to find out I am pouring out my life story to the long-lost love of my life! So, I will carry on tomorrow, promise!

Claudia logged out of Facebook, looked out at the night sky, and sighed. Had she said too much? She listened and watched as an ambulance siren punctuated the quiet night air and moved quickly up the road. Red blue. Red blue. Red blue.

She locked her office door and tiptoed into the house. Gareth was snoring softly in bed, and she carefully slipped in beside him. She closed her eyes and placed her hand over her heart. Alex. How could something that was so wrong feel so right?

The following morning, Claudia woke early and went through to her office, hoping that Alex had replied. Her heart skipped a beat when she found his unread message waiting for her.

13 August, 22:45 pm

Alex Winterton

No ways! There is absolutely no way that I was expecting you to reply tonight! Not only did you reply, but you quickly whipped up an intense response!

On the deep comments regarding you and me, I also felt the same and wondered "what if" many times, both during our time together as well as afterwards. Remember, nothing is ever too late. The Universe has a perfect sense of timing – always.

I think with us, we both had our hearts broken in different ways, but chatting to you now and fast-forwarding through the years has made it all so worthwhile and intriguingly interesting. I am really looking forward to catching up with you over time.

As for getting caught, I reckon there's a section in the Guinness Book of Records that we could enter and quite comfortably win.

Reading about your mom is so very sad. Have you allowed it to rest, or does this still sit heavily with you? It sounds like you really did do the best you could under all the circumstances and, in a little way, made the last years a bit more bearable for her.

Unfortunately, I don't have a great relationship with my mother. She has an exceptionally bad drinking problem, and the whole thing drives me crazy. I have tried talking to her, but I know that it is always the alcohol talking back. I know I am going to have to deal with this – and her – before it's too late, but it is a really big challenge for me.

Just a thought – it's so weird how we haven't spoken in years, and here we are both pouring our hearts out to one another and chatting like good old friends.

Until the morning then and the next time I hear from you, keep safe and sleep tight...

"Remember, nothing is ever too late..."

Claudia read the words over and over again, wondering what Alex had meant. Her mind was in a whirl.

14 August, 6:14 am

Claudia Stevenson

Alex, I totally agree with you about divine timing. Perhaps back then, the timing was just not right.

In terms of not having taken things further between us back then, I feel that I must clarify something with you: I slept with a guy I barely knew when I was in high school – long before you and I met and for totally stupid reasons. I think a lot of it stemmed from being insecure and looking for attention and affection in the wrong places. After I realised what I'd done, I made a promise to myself that the next person I took that step with would be the person I married, and I stuck to my guns on that one. It's a pity, though, in retrospect, we had some serious chemistry, and there probably would have been a lot of fireworks.

Perhaps in another lifetime, methinks.

Regarding my mom, yes, I have put it all to rest. She suffered for so many years, and her passing away was a relief, as much for me as it was for her. I do, however, have many regrets about the way she died, always wishing that I'd been closer to her at the time and that I'd been more of a daughter to her while I was growing up instead of being embarrassed about her and her disease. Unfortunately, I was only told about the Huntington's Disease by my dad when I phoned to tell him I was pregnant with Kyle, and he felt that I needed to know then because it was hereditary. It was very traumatic to suddenly have to undergo an amniocentesis, knowing that I might have to make a decision to terminate the pregnancy if Kyle had the gene. Fortunately, he was fine. I was tested for the disease after he was born, and I had not inherited the gene either.

I do miss having a mother around, though, and I never found that closeness with my stepmother, but that's all part of the big picture. Had I not been through what I went through and not had her as my mother, I would be in a very different place today.

I'm so sorry to hear about your mom! Was she drinking while you and I were together? I always thought there was something strange about her, but I never thought it was that. I completely understand where you are at. Gareth's dad is also an alcoholic, and it causes huge family stress. He doesn't realise how much his personality changes when he drinks and how he upsets everyone. I am always threatening to get a video camera out and film him in action so that he can see how much damage he does when he drinks.

I really feel for you. It's not a nice place to be. It's different when it's a friend – you can just cut them out of your life, but not when it's a parent.

My best friend's father died about eight years ago – he was also an alcoholic and died of cirrhosis of the liver. Not only was he a chronic alcoholic, but he was also a hobo. He lived on the street and ate from the hands of kind strangers. It was terrible.

You asked where Gareth and I met. We actually met at a New Year's party at a friend's house, but he was engaged to somebody else at the time. He broke his engagement off three months later, and we began dating. He was with me through all my troubles at home and helped me through so much that I would never have handled on my own. One thing led to another, and the next thing I knew, we were moving in together and planning a wedding a few years later.

He's a good person.

I was just re-reading your last message and thought how funny it is that we were both feeling the same about each other, yet neither of us did anything about it. It was as if there was never any closure between us. As I've said before, there was always something about us that kept you in a very special place in my heart. And just the fact that we can reconnect like this and just talk and talk and talk is quite incredible. Gareth would probably kill me if he knew, as he is the insanely jealous type.

I cannot wait to hear from you again.

Claudia thought about that *other life* she had referred to. Connecting with Alex on such a deep level was stirring up confusing thoughts and emotions in her heart. She knew that in a few hours, she would be receiving a new message from him, and she tossed and turned in bed that night, praying for the morning light to stream in through her bedroom window.

August 15th, 23:02 pm

Alex Winterton

Claudia, I must tell you that my focus has completely flown out of the window. I had a totally crazy day, in and out of meetings non-stop, and all I could think about was you and getting back to catching up. I was never this hooked on Facebook until now. It's like a drug, but it's the fix of you that I'm continually after.

I still cannot believe that we are actually chatting; it's really as if the years never happened. It feels like a very short time when, in fact, it's close to twenty years.

Occasionally, I have to pinch myself to check that I'm awake.

I still remember that last day when you told me you were breaking up with me. We walked from my place to the mall in silence, and your dad was there to fetch you. You drove off, and I just sat there for ages, not knowing what to think.

Claudia, you are somebody that I have never been able to forget. We had many special moments, both in the physical (even with getting caught) and in what I now see as the spiritual. Seventeen years later, there is still a deep connection between us. This is really deep for me, but I feel the energy of what I'm saying flowing through me right now as I type.

Thank you for your honesty and everything you have shared with me, both in the past and in the present.

As for sticking to the promise you made yourself, I am glad you did. As much as the mind and heart *wonder about what things might have been like, I know for sure that fireworks would have only been the beginning.*

Alex now sits and ponders that thought for some time...

It really sounds as if you and Gareth have a special relationship. His jealousy is probably only because he cares for and treasures the beautiful person he has in his life.

I would never want this renewed connection with us to come between the two of you in any way whatsoever. I hope I am clear on that. And if it ever potentially does, please let me know right away. I mean this, okay?

At this point, I am going to once again submit to my tiredness. There is so much that I want to respond to, and I promise to do so. There is also so much more that I want to hear. Until then, sleep tight.

Claudia's heart was thumping in her throat as she read and re-read Alex's words. He had *never* forgotten her, just as she had never forgotten him.

And as much as she tried to push the thought out of her mind, this was more than just a friendship that had resurfaced.

August 15th, 7:38 am

Claudia Stevenson

Alex, reading your words makes me wish you were right here and that I could just give you a long overdue hug. I really wish we'd been able to communicate more like this way back when we were seventeen.

I felt so sad reading about the time my dad fetched me from the mall, and you just sat there wondering why we had broken up. I remember that day, too. Part of me was devastated, but the other half longed to make things work.

I hope you don't mind me re-hashing all of this, but I really feel that so much has been left unsaid, and I've carried this with me for so many years.

When you sent me that first Facebook message asking me if I remembered you, I remember thinking to myself, how could I have forgotten you?

All these feelings are making me quite emotional. I'm just so amazed that what I thought was a one-sided connection for all these years has turned out to be a deeply two-sided one.

I shudder to think what would happen now if we had to bump into each other.

Thanks for everything you said about Gareth. Sometimes, the jealousy is totally overwhelming, and it is a huge stumbling block in our relationship. Even though I care for him deeply, I always think that jealousy stems from mistrust. Because of this, I feel that I cannot always tell him everything that is going on in my world because he might read into it the wrong way.

I don't think that Gareth would know how to deal with the knowledge that you and I have reconnected. He knows that you were a huge and special part of my life, and because of that, I think it would be safer to keep this information away from him for the time being.

Does Christine know that you and I are writing to each other?

I hope that there is no way that somebody could get their hands on these messages and blackmail us!

Gareth had no idea that anything was going on. He was so wrapped up in his own life and his own problems that he could not see beyond that. In the meantime, Claudia kept her distance and spent her hours trying desperately not to drift off into a fantasy world where it was just her and Alex, and everything was perfect.

August 16th, 12:35 am

Alex Winterton

My dearest Claudia,

Please feel free to hug as much as you would like to. For now, I will accept a virtual hug and return a massive one right back in your direction.

As for having been able to communicate like this while we were at school, I guess it is that whole cosmic timing element once again. I think that as one gets older (or, let's say, more mature), we get more in touch with who we are as a person and a spiritual being. I also think that inner truth comes more easily, and we also realise just how short life actually is. I, too, wish we had been more connected back then.

I always knew you were emotional, but I guess I probably missed the extent of it. Some of the things you have told me have made me look back in deep contemplation in an attempt to place it all in context.

Claudia, I am truly glad that you feel I am here for you emotionally in the present. It means so much to me, and in a way, it almost seems to make up for the past. I thank you for that, truly. If only you could feel the deep, intense feelings rushing through my body right now.

Please don't make the mistake or jump to the misconception, even for just one second, that I would not want to be sharing these special moments of our history with you. Our time together was really special for me, and being able to relive it like this is totally amazing and energising for my soul. I look forward to you sharing as much as you can and are able to.

I couldn't believe it when I found you on Facebook, but I honestly wondered if you would remember me. "Were we once?" was a bit of a cheesy heading for my introduction after seventeen years, but I guess it worked in terms of catching your attention.

I don't know about bumping into each other in this late stage of the game. If we were to meet now, I guess it would be due to a well-orchestrated arrangement. If we had bumped into each other before this reconnection, something says to me that we would have both been rather polite with one another, said the usual pleasantries, and then been on our way thinking, "Why didn't I take his (or her) number?" and "I wonder if I'll ever see him (or her) again?".

So, come to think of it, the way things have panned out between us has made everything rather interesting and intriguing.

Your feelings have most definitely not been one-sided at all. As I have said a few times, I have often wondered about you.

As for the jealousy thing, I know what you are saying there. I, too – funnily enough – am not the jealous type and with Christine, it has created some challenges. There have been many times where she has accused me of not caring at all. The truth is, I am a rather trusting person, and I don't believe that you can stop someone from doing something by being jealous.

As for Christine knowing about us, no, she doesn't, and I don't believe she would handle this well at all.

So, I guess you and I are in the same boat here.

There is something that I have been debating in terms of whether or not I should mention it, but I feel I need to. When I found you on Facebook, the first place I looked was at the pictures of you. The truth is that, unlike me, you have changed: you've gotten way more beautiful! I will admit to sitting and staring at your photos for quite some time...

It is now 00h31 as I finish this, and I will have to be up in three and a half hours. I also know that you should be coming through in about four and a half hours to check in on me and my reply.

I hope you are resting peacefully. It is almost the weekend, and I will have plenty of time to catch up with you then as well.

A brief goodbye until our next encounter...

The following morning, Claudia awoke, excited to read the magical lines that she knew had been left for her the night before.

As she read Alex's words, she felt both exhilarated and guilty. Claudia felt as if she was on a runaway train. The feelings and emotions were pouring out of her heart and her soul, and she felt in no way compelled to hold them back.

It was as if a web of magic had weaved its way into her life, and as much as she knew it was wrong, she smiled and submitted to its enchantment.

August 16th, 8:18 am

Claudia Stevenson

Alex, if it's any consolation, I couldn't get you out of my head yesterday. I tossed and turned the whole night, going over our time together and all the things you've said to me in the past couple of days and couldn't help thinking, "What if?"

You and I are similar in so many ways. I always knew there was a deep connection, even back then, but it seems as if we both needed to mature to be able to reconnect on the level we have now.

Alex (big breath as I say this), if you and I were not married, I can guarantee you that I would be sitting with you telling you all of this in person rather than typing it out. And I'm pretty sure you feel the same way. Just as you said in one of your letters, this is deep stuff, and I, too, can feel the energy of what I'm saying coursing through my veins as I type.

I just cannot believe that this is happening. So many years, so many feelings, so many things that should have been said and weren't, so many tears, and look at us now. I simply cannot get over this, and I'm not quite sure how to deal with all of my feelings right now.

I went back to the house before I started writing to you here, and I took my diary out of the cupboard again. I found so many pages in between the pages that I had not filled in, where I had just written and written about you. I had even stuck extra pages in to write on!

I was so in love with you then, Alex.

It is so funny how we have both got caught up in this conversation. It's amazing how we both feel this amazing energy between us.

I have been back to your photos on your Facebook page many times. It's good to see that you've looked after yourself and that you haven't turned out to be a beer-bellied thirty-four-year-old.

You are so right about the jealousy thing: being jealous only complicates things and invites mistrust into a relationship. If two people can be completely open and honest with each other, there should be no reason for jealousy. I sometimes wonder if it's also not a bit of possessiveness. What Christine says about you not seeming to care is what I hear all the time from Gareth. I am always honest with him and tell him that I do care, very much, in fact, but that it's very difficult to open my heart to him about my deepest feelings when he is going to be judgemental. I hate to say it, but I think that Gareth has become very insecure, both in and outside of our relationship. He uses money to buy things for himself to make him feel worthy on a material level, and he uses his harsh tongue to bring me down, and in a sad way, it probably gives him a sense of power and control over me.

Do you and Christine have a good relationship? I know I probably shouldn't be asking these things, but it's like I finally have the opportunity to get to know you really deeply again, and I want to know everything.

I have also been thinking that perhaps it is better that we keep things like this – virtual – there is way too much chemistry in the mix right now.

It is wonderful that you have developed a passion for writing. I'm an obsessive writer and can also express myself much better in writing than in person. I still want to write my own book one day. I am sure that there are many people out there, like us, who have reconnected and have the most incredible stories to tell. I have been thinking about writing a book called "The Facebook Diaries" and asking people to send me their stories. What do you think?

I cannot wait to hear from you again.

Just a few more hours, Claudia thought. Just a few more hours and Alex would be writing back to her again.

She felt giddy, as if she was standing on the edge of her life, arms outstretched, ready to fall forwards and let the wind catch her and swirl her up and around and float her gently down to earth and into Alex's arms.

August 17th, 9:23 am

Alex Winterton

Dearest Claudia, you are so dominating more and more of my thoughts and all in a damn beautiful way, especially while I drive. My mind normally runs off in all directions, but lately, I find myself thinking only of you.

There is so much I wish to tell you, as you already know, but I will get there.

Yes, the energy and blood racing through your veins. I know exactly what you mean because it is happening to me right now.

As for the feelings and the things that were left unsaid between us, I completely agree with the way you are feeling. I, however, look at it this way: You can either get stuck in the past and live in regret and miss out on the present, or you can learn from the past and totally live in the present each and every day and suck out the juice of each moment. This is my personal plan, and it's something I believe more of us need to do.

Take us, for example. I love this discussion we are sharing. It's so amazing, and sharing everything we have done and haven't done is wonderful. I do, however, sense that the "what ifs" pain you deeply, and I cannot allow that to happen to you.

I also wonder "what if" many times, but I know the reality is that no one (no matter who they are) can change the past. And besides that, the past happened for a reason. We were very different people back then. As you rightfully say, we were on different pages of life's book. I don't want there to be any pain for you, only joy. It is important that we focus on the great times we shared as that will only stand as a foundation to build on what you and I have once again found with each other.

Claudia, I know you loved me, as I truly loved you, but I honestly never got the sense of your love the way you portray it now. And for that, I guess I am truly sad.

There is so much that I still need to tell you, but I will have to leave you with this brief instalment for now until I write to you again.

With each reply, Claudia felt as if she was getting closer and closer to a new tipping point in her life.

She was trapped in a marriage that was destroying her, and she did not know how to break free from it. She felt so responsible for Gareth's happiness and could not bear to destroy his fragile state of mind. If anything, she was terrified of the repercussions of walking out of his life, which, in a sad, sadistic way, kept her bound to him and their life together. She had no idea of what this tipping point would bring. She knew that she was naïve to even think that she could ever be with Alex. He was married, too. It would take a miracle for them to be together.

The sadness crept into her heart, her soul aching for an answer.

August 17th, 11:12 am

Claudia Stevenson

Dearest Alex,

You are so right; the "what ifs" are very painful for me, especially knowing that there is still so much of life left to live, and I am now finding myself questioning my own happiness and wondering what choices I may have to make in the future. But I've decided that for now, I am going to, as you so rightly say, suck the juice out of this very special moment in my life.

The truth is, Alex, you were honestly one of the best things that ever happened to me, and for me, that is the hardest thing to deal with right now. Every other relationship I had after you, I would compare to our relationship, but none ever quite matched up to our good times and the intense feelings I had for you. You've always been in my heart for as long as I can remember, and I always thought to myself that if I were ever single one day, I would look you up, even if I was ninety years old with a Zimmer frame and false teeth!

I certainly didn't expect us to be writing to each other like this right now, each with another person, with our own lives, yet feeling as if all we want to be is together. So I guess that that really sucks a lot!

Gareth came into my life when I was in crisis mode. He's an amazing person, and I do love him deeply, but we are very different people from who we were when we met over a decade ago. Back then, we were both on the same level with the same ambitions and desires, but twelve years down the line, we are on completely different paths. I am more spiritual and grounded; he is more earthly and steeped in the past. I look on the bright side of life, while he tends to dwell on the negative. I offer a listening ear and advice where necessary, whereas he tends to be critical and judgemental. Things aren't the way they used to be, and it really makes me sad. I know that if things were perfect between Gareth and me, I would not have even contemplated having any kind of conversation with you at this stage in my life, never mind all the things I've said.

So when I talk about my own happiness, I look at things as they are right now and ask myself whether this is where I want to be in the next ten years. It's not as if Gareth and I haven't spoken about this; we talk about it almost every weekend – it's our only real time together. He knows how I long for more in a relationship, and he does try to meet my high standards, but at the end of the day, we are all who we are, and it's difficult to change yourself to please someone else.

I believe that if I just take one day at a time, everything will work out the way it should in the greater scheme of things...

I am sure that a time will come when we have caught up with each other completely, but then there will be the fun part of keeping up with the present and the future, so I cannot wait!

Later that afternoon, when her work day was done, Claudia busied herself by packing for a weekend away at their holiday home out in the country. Gareth whistled as he loaded one of the boy's quad bikes into the back of his truck, and she heard Kyle chattering away to his dad about all the fun they were going to have together over the weekend. Her precious boys. Claudia thought about Alex and her life with Gareth and her feelings for this man who had suddenly reappeared in her life. How was she going to spend a whole weekend with her husband and not let anything slip?

CHAPTER 3

Change does not whisper. It is not kind or mindful, nor is it respectful. Change is bold and brazen, like a bully, inviting itself in unannounced, and like a tsunami, it takes out everything in its path.

August 18th, 15:54 pm

Alex Winterton

Hey, girl!

One thing I need to really tell you before I continue is that I think your idea of writing a book called The Facebook Diaries is an amazing one. I cannot imagine how many other people have, like us, experienced the magic of a reconnection. Publishing their stories (even if they choose to remain anony-

mous) would be so exciting, and our story could be threaded in between.

But, back to the present.

I am glad I was spot on with what you were feeling and thinking, although it upsets me to think for even one second that you believe you had gone overboard in terms of your reply – because you didn't.

As for us and where this is all going, I am not sure, but I really love the way we are interacting at the moment, not to mention the depth and intensity of all the things we are sharing.

There is, however, something that is worrying me, and it unsettles me. Here goes:

I really hear the things you are telling me about you and Gareth, and I completely understand where you are coming from.

I am about to share something with you that might complicate things even more, but I don't want to in any way come between what both of you have built up over the last twelve years.

I couldn't live with myself or accept that.

Claudia, I am being completely honest with you right now as I type this. I can feel the blood rushing around my body and my internal temperature rise because it shakes me to my soul.

You asked me about myself and Christine. Well, the truth is that we have sadly come to the end of our journey together. It pains me, even as I type this to you, but it is something that I need to – and almost have – come to terms with. I love her very much and she is the only woman I have been with for as long as I have, but this is where we have both found ourselves. After knowing each other for close to nine years, and having the most amazing Native American wedding to bond us spiritually, I now dread the day we will be no more. We have spoken many times about where we are at and if we can retain what we have, and the only thing we feel that is left is an intense friendship. And it is that for which we are prepared to settle.

Because of this, the next while is going to be very emotional for me. There are so many areas of my life that are strong and successful, but this one is an area of weakness.

I have told nobody about this, and you are, therefore, the first person, outside of Christine and I, to know this. I am trying to be strong, and I am continually working on my strength. I honestly believe that this will be a good time of growth for me, and I have started preparing myself mentally and emotionally for it.

So once again, although I have shared this very deep secret with you, it is really important to me that you don't let any of this cloud your judgment. And knowing where you are (only because the discussions that you and Gareth have had sound very similar to the ones that Christine and I have had), I would urge you to sit him down and really get him to understand your feelings and what you really need, both as a soul and as a woman. Don't think of giving up too easily. Promise me that? I know what I am talking about. You need to fight hard for the things you believe in, and I believe if you want something badly enough, you can have it.

Besides, I am more than happy to wait until you are ninety years old. I haven't ever really had much of an issue with false teeth; I actually find the whole thing quite sexy, in a we-can-share-each-other's-teeth kind of way. Besides, by then, there should be some really cool technology around that would make the whole thing very interesting for people that age.

Jokes aside, I mean what I am saying to you – I honestly do.

Claudia sat rooted to her chair, staring at her laptop screen in utter disbelief. Gareth was playing tennis with a friend, and the boys were in the room next door playing PlayStation. She read and reread Alex's words. Suddenly, everything had changed. Where an opportunity once before seemed too out of reach to grab on to, it had now moved forward like a knight on a chessboard, leaping over obstacles and taking out everything in its path.

Her world was shifting on its axis, and she was powerless to stop it.

Her mind was in a whirl, and she had to hold on to the edge of the table she was sitting at to steady herself. She felt dizzy. Elated. Terrified.

Could this be her chance to escape from her reality for real?

Claudia knew that Gareth was going to be returning soon, but she wanted to reply to Alex more than anything.

With trembling hands and one eye watching out of the window for Gareth's return, Claudia quickly typed a reply to Alex.

August 18th, 18:04 pm

Claudia Stevenson

Alex! My hands are shaking, and my heart is racing. I feel as if I'm about to pass out!

I never thought I was going to hear the things you've just said.

I am so grateful that you have shared such intimate details of your life with me. I wish that I was at the point that you are at with Christine. In a strange way, I actually envy you.

This is just totally incredible. I never in my wildest dreams thought a day like this would ever come. It feels as if the Universe has opened up a path for us to be together.

Claudia heard the rumble of a car's engine in the driveway and looked up. It was Gareth. Claudia was still shaking. She quickly closed her laptop, looked up at him, and smiled weakly as he walked in through the door carrying a few bags of shopping.

"I've invited Grace and Charlie over for dinner tonight," he said. "I'm going to make a fire for a barbeque."

Grace and Claudia had been close friends for many years, and Grace had often been a first-hand witness to Claudia and Gareth's tumultuous marriage. She was the first person that Claudia had called when she had received the "*Were we once?*"

message. She had no idea how deep the relationship had progressed since that day.

As Claudia busied herself by preparing a salad for the evening's meal, Grace breezed in through the front door carrying a bottle of wine.

"Hey you," she said, smiling while she uncorked the bottle of wine. "Why the serious face?"

Claudia took a long sip and breathed in deeply.

"Shit, my friend, you have no idea what kind of trouble I've got myself into."

"Do you still love Gareth?" Grace asked reflectively after she had listened, wide-eyed, to everything Claudia had revealed. "I mean, if you are still in love with him, it's one thing, but if you're not, and you want to get out, then that changes everything."

Claudia excused herself from the barbeque later that evening, taking her laptop with her into the bathroom, hoping for something, anything, from Alex. And sure enough, there it was...

August 18th, 20:51 pm

Alex Winterton

Claudia, I need to clear something up: There is nothing to envy about where Christine and I are at. It is extremely painful and difficult for both of us, and we are trying so hard to work things out. And once again, just because of where I am, I don't want it to affect you and Gareth or for me to come between the two of you. Please understand that.

I look forward to your replies later when you have a chance. Please be sure not to cause any unnecessary suspicion, as this wouldn't be good for either of us right now.

Claudia felt the blood rush to her cheeks as she cringed internally. She had let go of her emotions and had come on too strong. In her heart, she knew that there was every possibility that she had sent Alex running for the hills.

She had to let him know that she was sorry, that there was still the present to deal with, and that was emotionally upsetting enough without a long-lost girlfriend professing her undying love...

❦

August 18th, 21:14 pm

Claudia Stevenson

Oh, Alex, I'm sure you must think that I am callous and unfeeling, which is not the case.

Let me start again.

When I say that I envy your situation, it's not because I want to be there right now. I envy you because you and Christine have both been mature enough to realise that your relationship is not going anywhere. You have worked hard and put so many years into your marriage, but it takes a strong person to accept that things aren't working.

In my case, it's different. I am nowhere near as happy in my marriage as I want to be, and I cannot imagine spending the rest of my life wishing that I had walked away from the relationship sooner.

Gareth and I have tried hard to work things out, but what I keep realising is that if your heart is not in something, it's never going to work. The situation I find myself in right now is also extremely painful, and I can empathise with what you're going through with Christine. It's not that easy to walk away from, in your case, six years of marriage.

In my situation, Gareth seems to think that things will ultimately work out between us. To be honest, it is such a horrible situation – I no longer love him the way I used to. From my side, it is more platonic, yet he practically worships the ground I walk on. I need space to grow, whereas he smothers me. I hope you don't think I'm sounding arrogant because I'm not – it's just the way it is. Truthfully, he deserves more than what I am able to offer. I just wish he'd see that. He's forever telling me how so-and-so does this and how so-and-so does that, and why am I not like that, and why can't I just change and be the person he wants me to be – the person I was sixteen years ago. I keep telling him that I am not the same person he met all those years ago: insecure with very little self-confidence, confused and alone. I have grown up, and I'm a completely different person.

Please don't think that you are possibly coming between Gareth and me. That is not the case at all. Things have been messy for over two years now. We struggle to see eye to eye with most things, and sometimes, I think we're only together because of the common bond we share, our children.

Whatever path our circumstances are leading us on is exactly where we need to be right now. I must admit that having you appear out of the woodwork, reading your messages, loving the person you've become, and reminiscing over our past together, makes me very happy and excited at the possibility of our new found connection.

And as I've said before, had my marriage been solid, I would never have said the things to you that I've said. Please understand me when I say this.

I know that your heart must be aching and torn between sticking it out or going it alone. I know that

that is something I, too, will have to deal with one day soon, and it scares the hell out of me. When you build your life with someone and share so much with them, it's not that easy to just give it all up, even more so when there are children involved.

My boys love their father dearly, and he spoils them rotten. It breaks my heart to think of the day that I might have to tell them that our family structure is going to be changing. I am trying to be a little bit selfish and not worry about everyone else's feelings, but it is incredibly hard, and I know it is going to take me a long time to come to terms with whatever decision I decide to make.

So, just so that you know, I am here for you, more than you know, and I will be travelling along this new path in your life and lifting you up whenever you need me to.

Claudia clicked on the send button, closed her laptop and quietly opened the bathroom door. She watched Ross's chest slowly rising and falling as he slept peacefully in front of the television.

She covered him with a blanket and walked back outside to join her husband and her friends.

The tsunami had left as quickly as it had entered. Claudia could feel the particles in her life separating, and her mind was abuzz with thoughts of what-ifs and what-nows.

It was with peace in her heart and a sense of new found hope that she read Alex's message to her later that night…

August 18th, 22:32 pm

Alex Winterton

Claudia, let me begin by saying thank you to you for your message and for setting the record straight. It is important to me to know that where you are at has nothing to do with me or what we have found in reconnecting.

When you were telling me how you are not the person you once were (sixteen years before), I found myself thinking about how different and mature you must be now. I mean, you look the same (only way hotter) – okay, I never said that, but you sound so different from how I remember you.

I am so happy to have reconnected with you and to have an opportunity to get to know you in a way I possibly would not have had, had our paths not crossed the way that they did in the past month.

Sometimes, the healing begins when we are able to accept what is and move on. The heart cannot mend until the head is in the right place. Our path to happiness cannot open up until we clear the brambles out of the road.

Claudia could only hope that when she turned the corner, Alex would still be waiting there for her.

CHAPTER 4

In the days that followed, Alex and Claudia's connection intensified. They were in the centre of a perfect storm, both knowing that at any minute, the walls around them could come crashing down.

Both were aware of the dangerous ground they were treading on, particularly Claudia, who knew that with every word she exchanged with Alex, she was one step closer to the tipping point in her marriage.

Claudia wanted nothing more than to run – to pack her bags, close the front door, get into her car, and drive away from the life that no longer served her, but she knew that could never happen. She was shackled to the contract of an empty, failed marriage, and she knew that Gareth would no sooner kill her than let her go.

Alex was acutely aware of the risk of any deeper contact, be it in the flesh or otherwise. He ached to dial her number, to hear her voice as she answered the telephone, and to simply say, "*Guess who?*"

In an attempt to ground himself, he started sculpting a work of art in the background, a picture of a time when they would be reunited, free from the shackles of their past, an erotic love thriller of epic proportions.

August 20th, 20:51 pm

Alex Winterton

My darling Claudia, I really struggled to sleep last night – I had thoughts of you running through my head, and I kept tossing and turning. I cannot even begin to explain this tantalising excitement that has flooded my core since you came back into my life.

There is this weird thing going on with Christine of late: I have really been battling with my feelings and have been very conscious of hers, trying to give her the strength she needs (there is a very long story here, and this one I will only tell you in person), but over the past couple of days she has been picking up on my stronger sense of self, and it is making her feel very uneasy. Right now, as I am typing this, I am not sure if I should be telling you this – I feel as if I am betraying her by doing so.

Today, we had a bad exchange. I had to come home early because she had gone into what seemed like a deep depression. We spoke, and there were tears, and then we spoke some more. As I was saying, though, I kept thinking of you. I think it's all the things we were chatting about, especially all the stuff from Saturday and Sunday; it was truly deep and involved.

I must still mention to you – and I know we have touched on this, and you need not reply, but I just need to get it out there – but it really does pain me that you and Gareth are not one hundred percent in your happy place. It is really sad when couples lose that connection and just can't make it work beyond a point.

I'll be hanging around here for the next while, hoping that I might see something from you.

By the way, do you use Skype?

August 20th, 22:07 pm

Claudia Stevenson

Do I use Skype? What I wouldn't do to hear your voice. I have little electric prickles going through my body just imagining it.

Having said that, though, we would have to be very careful if we took the step to chat in a live environment...

August 20th, 22:19 pm

Alex Winterton

Don't worry. I wouldn't phone you online. I think the pressure would be immense, and I wouldn't put you through that. We can just type to each other.

Send me your details, and I'll do the rest.

Claudia felt as if she had taken a freefall dive off a cliff. She sent Alex a contact request, and within seconds, Alex's first real-time message appeared on her screen.

Alex: *Hey you!*

Claudia: *Oh my God, there you are! This feels so surreal.*

Alex: *Well, my sexy cyber soul mate, this is totally real and happening.* Claudia: *Never in my wildest dreams did I ever think we'd be talking to each other like this.*

Alex: *Me neither. But I am glad we are.*

Claudia: *Alex, I really want to say how sorry I am about what happened between you and Christine today. It doesn't sound good.*

Alex: *Thank you. I appreciate that. It's all pretty intense at the moment, but I guess we are both focussed on the end goal, and we can't allow ourselves to become derailed in the process.*

Claudia: *Gareth and I have said about ten words to each other tonight. We're miles away from the end goal!*

Alex: *Are you sure things can't improve for you and Gareth?*

Claudia: *Alex, I don't know, honestly. I actually don't know how to even begin to explain. I am caught between a rock and a hard place, literally. I keep thinking that moving out to the countryside will fix everything, but the more I think about it and the dynamics of our marriage, the more I know that it is not the solution. There are deeper issues which neither of us see eye to eye on. The only com-*

mon goal we share at the moment is selling our house, building our dream house, and our children, and we hardly see eye to eye over them either. It's just so damn tiring. He wants me to love him, but I can't. There's no love left. There's nothing about him that excites me anymore. It's so sad to have to say it, but I really believe that he deserves better – someone who is more on his wavelength than I am.

Alex: *You know what, this is so weird... your words describe exactly what Christine feels about our marriage.*

Claudia: *I feel guilty sitting here talking to you (even though I love it so much) because I wish I could be talking to him like this, but it's like there is this huge brick wall that I've built up between him and me.*

Alex: *I wish things weren't so complicated. I mean, you feel that you need more from Gareth, and Christine feels she needs more from me. I know in my heart I have tried all I can and then some. How does a person turn things around?*

Claudia: *I've been trying to fix things for years, Alex. I'm not a difficult person, but I cannot tolerate the verbal abuse any longer. I don't know if it's possible to turn things around. Even our friends have picked up on Gareth and I. Everyone can see what is going on. Gareth simply won't accept that he is just as responsible for this mess as I am.*

Alex: *I know that feeling. The thing that is in my space the most is that we will eventually have so many people to tell – people who have always known us as a couple.*

Claudia: *Yes, I know, that is going to be difficult. Shit, it's hectic. I wish I could wave a wand and have this all behind me. Right now, I'm worried about how this is going to impact everybody's lives. It is so damn scary.*

Alex: *Okay, guess what? I refuse to allow either of us to go off to bed on this extremely solemn note, so let's both close our eyes and send each other a virtual hug.*

Claudia: *You'll have to give me a second to mop up the tears.*

Alex: *No, now come on, my sexy cyber soul mate, I can't have you being upset. Now, close your eyes.*

Claudia: *Eyes are closed.*

Alex: *Imagine me kissing you on each of your eyelids. Feel my love for you right now.*

Claudia: *That's beautiful, Alex. Thank you.*

Alex: *You're so welcome.*

Alex: *PS... I sifted through your photos on Facebook tonight.*

Claudia: *Oh yes? And?*

Alex: *It was such fun, actually. You have really beautiful boys.*

Claudia: *Thank you, Alex. You are one gorgeous human being, do you know that?*

Alex: *Thank you! You're pretty special yourself.*

Claudia: *I wish you could see the smile on my face right now.*

Alex: *I can feel it.*

Alex: *Okay, don't make me beat you. Off to bed with you!*

Claudia: *Okay then, sweet dreams, you sweet person.*

Alex: *Night, night*

Claudia locked the door to her office and walked upstairs. She knelt down beside Ross and Kyle as they lay sleeping in their beds and kissed them both on their foreheads. She hated herself for the double life she was living, and deep down, she knew that there was going to come a time when enough was enough – something had to give.

She woke up the next morning, and Gareth rolled over and looked her in the eyes.

"You're the best thing that ever happened to me, Claudia," he said sleepily.

August 21st, 7:25 am

Claudia Stevenson

Alex, I cannot begin to tell you how much you are consuming my thoughts. The more I think about you, the more I have to pinch myself to remind myself that you are real. You are still the same boy that I fell in love with all those years ago, yet you seem so different. I really love the person you have become.

I know we went over Christine and you and Gareth and I last night, but I must just say once again how freaky it is that we are basically sitting in the same situation, both feeling guilty because of the strength we are drawing from each other. It is immensely powerful, so much so that I think we both feel that we almost have an edge over our situations.

Gareth knows something is up. This morning, he told me that I was the best thing that ever happened to him. Why would he say something like that when deep down he is so unhappy in our marriage? He's always moaning about how much I've changed. He says he's proud of who I've become but can't understand why there's no closeness between us, even though I've told him why so many times. I swear he thinks I'm making things up.

On Friday night, we went out for pizzas with the boys, and I bumped into a friend who is going through a divorce but who seemed incredibly happy. I was telling Gareth about her, and he looked at me and said, "Is that what you want? A divorce?"

So I said, "Maybe, or perhaps a six-month break".

He laughed and said that there was no way in hell that I could live without him for six months.

Sometimes, I think he is so conceited.

August 21st, 9:55 am

Alex Winterton

Falling asleep last night was no easy task at all. Thoughts of you consumed me, too.

Young lady, seventeen years ago, I was a young and immature punk with very little, if any, focus at all. It was all about going out with mates and getting as drunk as possible. Today, you are being *re-introduced to a well-groomed, intelligent, keenly focused young man.*

As for the spouse's saga, I sense your frustration, and for that, I am truly sorry, but at the same time, I am glad that we can share this part of our lives with each other.

I am so happy with us right now. In fact, you have no idea...

August 21st, 18:10 pm

Claudia Stevenson

I like the description of the New You. I didn't quite ever see you as the young, immature punk you described, but I totally love the man you have become!

You think you're happy? I'm totally and blissfully elated. I am still pinching myself that we're here – that you're here, in my life, in a way that I never dreamed possible.

It was hardly noticeable at first, but the pounding walls that surrounded the eye of that perfect storm had begun to gain momentum.

Tips of white were forming on the crests of the waves that surrounded Alex and Claudia as they tried to escape. Escape from their current lives. To see the sun shine again. To feel the gentle breeze of the ocean dance between them.

The sky grew dark, and the sun clenched her golden rays into her fist. The black swan had begun its approach...

CHAPTER 5

Two lives hanging in the balance, like the metal balls suspended from a frame in a Newton's Cradle. Click. The sound as one ball swings and collides with the others. Silence. Stillness. The energy flows through, and suddenly, the ball at the end lifts and swings and collides back on itself. Click. And the energy flows backwards again.

A soul will always remain at rest until it is acted upon by another force.

August 22nd, 12:45 am

Alex Winterton

Good morning, gorgeous!

So, I promised you a little something, and here it is:

I'd like you to close your eyes and imagine the following...

White desert beach sand. A moonless night sky sprinkled with stars that glimmer in a crescendo of dark to white light. The sound of waves crashing against the shoreline and the silence as the tide pulls them back in again.

Your feet are bare and sunken into the cool, soft sand. The warm summer night air tickles your skin, and you feel your dress brush against your thighs.

You smile to yourself and turn around to make your way to our room. You watch the flickering of the candles dance in unison with the rhythm of your soul.

You find a beautifully lit, sensual, pulsating Jacuzzi. You slowly remove your dress and slip into the warm water. You feel the jets pound against your soft skin. You close your eyes and tilt your head backwards, taking in the warmth and peace that surrounds you.

You open your eyes sleepily as you sense my presence in the room. I hold out an open towel to you, and as you rise, I wrap it around your soft, sweet-smelling skin and slip you into a soft, silky gown that flows over your body.

I place my arm around your waist and lead you through to the master bedroom, where soft, relaxing music plays in the background. As you lay down on the bed, I rub a combination of sweet-smelling oils into my hands and begin to massage your body, starting with your back and neck, then your legs and arms and finally your feet and hands. I can feel you drift in and out of a tranquil sleep as my hands caress your body.

I gently touch those parts of your body that I have craved to touch for so long. I can sense that you are aching for me, and my body tingles as you reach out and open the wrap that covers my waist.

Our bodies press against each other, lips and tongues collide, and as you look up into my eyes, I feel our souls connect. We move in unison, our hearts racing, our souls entwined, our bodies as one.

The suppressed yearning and hunger that each of us has carried for all these years melts into a frenzy of passion that neither has experienced before, and we both gasp for air as the fever consumes us and sends us soaring over the edge of reason into unbridled ecstasy.

Lying in each other's arms and gazing into one another's eyes, the morning light teases her way through the curtains and plays with the dark locks of hair that have fallen across your face. We smile at each other, knowing that, at last, the missing puzzle pieces in our lives have found their way home.

The End

Desperation. Disillusionment. Longing. Escape.

Reading Alex's message sent shockwaves through Claudia's body. She felt as if she was about to pass through a thin veil into an alternate universe.

Everything felt completely and utterly surreal.

August 22nd, 7:25 am

Claudia Stevenson

Alex, you amaze me more and more every day. Just when you've blown me away with one thing, you have me panting over another! I pictured everything so clearly. I could actually see us there together. I could feel your body close to mine, the heat between us as you wrapped that towel around me. I could feel the stifled breathing. I could feel your hands rubbing up and down my body, and I could feel my body arching as the delicious sensations rippled through my very being. You have no idea how you're making me feel. If I were a man, I would be wearing a really baggy pair of pants right now.

I hardly slept last night, and yes, I was very tempted to come down to the office and see what you'd written. But there is something exciting about waking up with the sun peeking over the horizon, knowing that my real sunshine has written something beautiful for me, so I let the suspense drag out a bit.

Right now, it feels as if without us, nothing else would be happening. I feel as if I have this amazing power, that nothing can touch me right now.

All I want to do is be with you, and I am starting to wonder how much more of this I can take before I crack.

Claudia clicked the send button and sat back in her chair, running her fingers through her hair. At that moment, she felt as if she was balancing on a sword's edge, about to be torn in two between loyalty and love. The pain was so great and so unbearable, and she felt like screaming out in agony.

Gareth stormed into her office, waving a piece of paper about.

"I've asked you a hundred times already," he yelled. "When are you going to call the municipality and sort this mess out?"

Claudia felt her soul and her body collide as she was sucked back to reality at the sound of Gareth's voice.

"Gareth, I'm running my own business. I'm not your secretary," she protested. "Can't you just sort your own stuff out? This is your account, not mine."

"I'm so sick of you, Claudia," he continued. "Always passing the buck when it comes to anything that has something to do with me. I do so much for you. Honestly, I don't know why I am even married to you."

Claudia baulked. She had heard those lines so many times before and had always responded in the same kind, gentle way, never wanting to disappoint her children, her family, his family, and most importantly, herself by having to label herself and the lives of her children with the dreaded "D" word.

But this time was different. It was as if she had been chained to a pole her whole life, and each time Gareth had threatened her with divorce, she had pulled away from the pole, but she'd never been strong enough to set herself free. This time, however, it felt as if a weak link in the chain had been exposed, that she just had to tug on it one more time, just one more time, and it would snap, and she would fall and stumble and lift herself up off the ground and run away from everything as fast as she could; run away into the arms of the man she'd loved all her life.

"Are you asking me for a divorce, Gareth?" she asked as she sighed, feeling a sense of emptiness clouding her voice. "Because if that's what you want, you can have it. It's all yours. Take your ticket to freedom and run because I'm tired of you, and I'm tired of this marriage, and I want out."

She felt her eyes well up with tears, shocked that she had summoned the power within her soul to utter those words but, at the same time, relieved that she had.

Gareth stormed out of the office, furious. Confused. Sad.

"Fuck you, Claudia," he yelled back at her. "Fuck you!"

He went upstairs and pulled a suitcase from the top shelf and stood motionless as he lost his grip on the handle, and it fell heavily to the floor. His hands were shaking. He stared blankly at the shelves of clothes in front of him. *Could this really be happening? Was Claudia really being serious? Was it really over?*

He zipped open the suitcase and swept his clothes off the shelves into it. He could feel his jaw aching as he clenched his teeth. No, it couldn't be over. He didn't really mean it. Surely she knew that he was just trying to scare her?

A feeling of panic overcame him, and he stopped what he was doing and ran back down the stairs and into the office. Claudia looked up at him, not sure what to say or think. The look on his face scared her.

"Can we talk about this in the house," he said quietly, not wanting Claudia's staff to hear what was going on. "Now, please."

Claudia nodded and followed Gareth back to the house, her heart pounding uncontrollably in her chest. Her mind was in a whirl. She had a way out, but suddenly it felt as if she had driven her car off a bridge into a lake, and the car was slowly filling up with water. She was suffocating, and although she could see the sun and the sky outside, she wasn't sure if she had the strength to pry the door open and swim to the surface.

"Are you sure about this?" he asked as they stood facing each other.

Claudia swallowed hard and nodded.

"Gareth, it's time. You know as well as I do that this isn't working. I am never going to be the wife you want me to be – you keep telling me that. Every time we argue, you ask for a divorce. Why is it different this time?"

"I don't want to lose you, Claudia," pleaded Gareth. "I'm sorry. I don't know what came over me. I didn't mean what I said. I love you. Please, can we try to work this out?"

Claudia felt the darkness closing in on her and fought against it with every fibre of her being. She wasn't going to drown. Not this time.

In her mind, she pictured Alex and the future that they might now be able to have together. She had lost him once. She wasn't going to let him slip through her fingers again.

"Are you leaving me for Denise?" she heard him ask, the feeling of suffocation closing in on her like a thick mist, it's icy fingers running up her back and tightening around her throat.

"No, Gareth," Claudia said, sighing as she caught her reflection in the mirror behind him. "It's not Denise. I just can't do this anymore. Can't you just accept that things are over between us?"

Claudia watched as Gareth's face darkened. She was acutely aware of the pain that was tearing through his heart, but she knew that if she backed out now, she would have surrendered her one and only opportunity to release herself from his grip.

He walked out of the room, slamming the door behind him. She heard him pick up his car keys, and she shivered as he yelled back at her, "I'm fetching the children from school. And you're going to tell them that you're about to ruin their lives!"

Her ears were ringing, and her heart was pounding. She paced the room while she waited for him to return home with their children. She thought of Alex. She thought about Denise. She desperately tried not to picture her children's faces when she broke the news to them. She was reeling with the heaviness of the responsibility of being the one to shatter their innocent lives.

Alex. She desperately needed to tell him what was going on. Claudia quickly typed a message to him explaining what had just happened. She felt as if she was slipping on a knife's edge.

When Gareth returned home, he told the children to go downstairs with Claudia and wait for him. Claudia's skin prickled as she heard his footsteps coming down the spiral staircase. Every step that he took symbolised a step closer to one world ending and another beginning.

Ross and Kyle sat quietly, unsure of the reason for this strange family gathering. Gareth sat down and looked directly into Claudia's eyes.

"Go on then," he said, "Tell them what you've done."

Claudia frowned, and she felt the tears welling up in her eyes.

"My boys," she whispered between stilted sobs. "Your father and I are getting divorced."

She gulped as she watched their eyes widen.

"I'm so sorry," she continued, her voice shaking. "But please know that we're both going to still be in your lives, and we're going to make sure that this is not too difficult for you. I promise that with all my heart and soul."

Kyle, in absolute shock and disbelief, had tears streaming down his little face. Ross whimpered, unable to comprehend what was being discussed. As a six-year-old, the word "divorce" was foreign to his vocabulary.

Claudia heard the ruffling of a plastic bag, and she moved her focus away from the boys towards Gareth. He was standing now and walked towards the boys carrying two heavy wads of elastic-bound cash notes in his hands. Bewildered, Claudia watched in slow motion as he handed each child one of these bundles.

"My boys," he said, "take this cash and go and buy yourselves something special with it. I hope it's enough. I'm so sorry. I love you guys."

He turned and placed one of his hands on the railing of the staircase.

"This is the last time that you will ever see me," he said, his eyes darting between Claudia and the boys. "And you," he said in what sounded like a growl from a person possessed by a demon, "you, Claudia, have blood on your hands, and you're not welcome at my funeral."

With that, he turned and walked up the staircase. Claudia drew her children close, staring in blank disbelief at the empty space in which he had stood so resolute just a few minutes before, and she felt a strange feeling of anger welling up in her belly.

"How dare he?" she thought to herself, fighting back the tears. "He's fucking crazy!"

She had heard him make idle threats, although not as dramatic as this one, during their tumultuous marriage, and she wondered what on earth to make of this one. In that moment, it felt as if the world had stopped spinning, and an eerie silence crept into the room, enveloping Claudia and her children.

"What did he mean, Mommy," asked Kyle. "What did he mean when he said you've got blood on your hands?"

Claudia breathed in deeply and sighed, wiping the tears from Kyle's face, "I don't know, my darling, I don't know. But don't be scared. I will protect both of you. I won't let anything happen to you. Daddy's just angry. Everything will be okay."

CHAPTER 6

Everything felt surreal. Claudia's head felt as if it was on the spin cycle of a washing machine. Should she take him seriously this time? Was the blood really on her hands? What was Gareth talking about? Why would he say something so heartless in front of his children? The questions whirled around in her head as she took the boys upstairs.

She walked into the kitchen and caught the scent of the chicken casserole that was bubbling away in the slow cooker. She had prepared it that morning before the confrontation. Claudia wondered how many people would be sitting down for dinner in their home that night.

She turned around and picked up her mobile phone. She had to speak to Gareth's sister Jody. Jody was probably the most neutral person in the family, and Claudia thought that she had a right to know what was going on.

She started dialling Jody's number and stopped. She had to phone Gareth. She was going to go out of her mind if she didn't speak to him and at least try to bring him to his senses. Nothing made sense. She walked to the front door and found a pile of suitcases strewn across the floor. She looked out of the window, half expecting to see his car parked in the driveway. The gate had been left open, but the car was gone.

She remembered her phone. She dialled Gareth's number and held her breath. She leaned up against the wall, feeling its coolness penetrate her skin.

"Oh God, please answer, please, please answer," she said quietly under her breath, hoping the boys wouldn't hear her desperate pleas.

Gareth's phone rang on the other side. Claudia counted the rings. One. Two. Three. Four. Five. "Oh God," she thought. Five. Six. Voicemail.

She tried again. Voicemail.

The third time she called, the call was answered, but instead of his voice, Claudia could hear a song playing in the background. It was quiet at first, and Claudia struggled to make out what song it was, but then she felt her blood go cold. The volume intensified, and she heard the chorus of the song she and Gareth had fallen in love with just a few weeks earlier after watching Gwen Stefani perform it live for the first time at The Grammys, screened across the world on live television. *Four in the Morning*. It was about giving everything that she had and handing over everything that she was because she didn't want to give up on true love.

She felt her hands tremble as the phone clicked on the other side. What was he trying to tell her?

She dialled his number again. This time, the volume was blaring. And the words came down the line again.

"Gareth!" she pleaded down the phone. "Please, Gareth, stop whatever it is that you're doing. Please!"

The phone clicked again, and there was silence. Claudia was trembling uncontrollably. She felt sick to her stomach. She dialled his number again. Once again, the haunting words played for her.

Claudia shouted down the line, "Gareth! Please! It's enough now! You're acting crazy! Please stop."

Again, the call was terminated.

Claudia felt her knees bending and her back sliding down the wall until she felt the floor beneath her. She realised she was gasping for air. She heard the feint sound of the television playing upstairs and realised that Kyle and Ross were probably watching a movie. "Thank God," she whispered under her breath. "This is beyond crazy."

She decided to try one more time. She had to get through to him. He was scaring her. He was messing with her mind. It felt like emotional blackmail, and if it was, she thought, it was certainly working.

Gareth picked up the phone before it had a chance to ring on her side. There was no more music, just the sound of his laboured breathing on the other end of the line.

"Gareth," Claudia pleaded, her hands shaking. "Let's just forget about what happened this morning. Please, just come home and let's work things out. Things don't have to be like this. The children are worried about y…"

He cut her off in mid-sentence.

"I'll never take you back," he hissed. "I'll never take you back!"

There was silence on the other end.

That familiar click as he ended the call again.

Frantic with worry, she called him back, but this time, there was no answer, no music, just his voicemail.

"Hi, you've reached Gareth. Leave me a message after the beep, and I'll get back to you."

She tried again. And again. There was only voicemail.

Jody.

"Claudia?" she heard Jody's voice on the other end of the line.

"Jody, please come over. I'm scared. It's Gareth."

"I'm on my way," she said. "I'll be there as fast as I can."

Claudia couldn't get the song out of her head. She couldn't understand what Gareth was trying to tell her, and she sure as hell didn't know what his next move was going to be.

Frustration, confusion, anger. It was difficult to tell how she felt.

She sat for what felt like hours, her mind foggy and clouded in uncertainty. Through the fuzziness, she heard footsteps coming through the front door.

"Claudia!' It was Jody's voice. "Oh my God, why are Gareth's things strewn across the floor like this?"

Claudia crossed her legs on the floor and looked up at her sister-in-law.

"Did Gareth call you this morning, Jody?"

"Nope," replied Jody matter-of-factly. "But he did go through to Mom and Dad. He was really upset. He said you wanted a divorce. Is it true?"

"Well, yes and no," sighed Claudia, and proceeded to share the morning's events with Jody. "He came home with the boys, dished some cash out to them, told me I had blood on my hands, that I wasn't welcome at his funeral, and then he left. I've tried calling him, but all he does is answer the phone with a song blaring down the microphone, and now he won't answer his phone at all. I'm really scared, Jody. I think he's going to try to hurt himself."

Jody retrieved her phone from her handbag and dialled Gareth's number. Voicemail.

"Shit."

"I know."

"Does he have a vehicle tracking device in his car," asked Jody. "Maybe they can get a location on his vehicle."

"You know, I think he does," said Claudia, suddenly hopeful. "Let me get the paperwork with his account details."

Claudia rummaged through his box of filing, pulling out an invoice. A telephone number and an account number. That was all she needed.

She dialled the control room.

"Satnav, how can we help you?"

The situation suddenly felt incredibly surreal. Claudia had been her husband's bookkeeper for years and had captured the debit order transaction for Satnav every month. Not for one second did she ever think she would be making this call. Satnav was there for vehicle theft and hijackings, not deranged husbands who were trying to scare the shit out of their wives.

Claudia cleared her throat. "Um, yes, yes, please. My husband has gone missing, and I'm trying to track him down. Would you be able to help me find him? He left the house a couple of hours ago, and I cannot reach him."

The voice had gone quiet on the other side.

"Sure, ma'am, okay," it came back. "Just give me your account number, and I'll use it to get a location on your husband."

Claudia's heart was thumping so loudly in her chest that she thought she could see it physically beating through her shirt. She gulped and looked at Jody, covering the mouthpiece, "He's going to tr…"

"Ma'am, just give me a couple of minutes," the voice came through again. "You'll have to hold on, but I've found your husband's details on the system. I'm just waiting for my technicians to bounce a signal off the car so that we can determine exactly where he is."

Claudia thanked him and then put her hand back over the mouthpiece and whispered to Jody: "They're going to see if they can pick up a signal from his car. Oh God, I hope he is okay."

Jody looked at Claudia, and Claudia could see the terror welling up in the tears that filled his sister's eyes. Jody knew that Gareth was unstable at the best of times. They'd had their share of arguments in the past, and Jody had often been witness to his idle threats. Gareth had never felt good enough for anyone. Not even himself.

"Ma'am?" It was the voice again. "Ma'am, this is strange but not entirely abnormal, but we can't pick up a signal on your husband's car."

"Shit," said Claudia, "I'm sorry. What exactly does that mean?"

"Look," said the voice, "he may just be out of range. I don't know how long he's been go…"

"It's been three hours already," Claudia interrupted.

"Okay, well then, there are two scenarios. One is that he has driven far out into the country, and he's off our radar, but what is more likely is that he is parked underground, in a building or perhaps even at a hotel. The concrete slabs in underground parking lots often make the signal difficult to pick up."

The voice paused. "But what I'll do is I'll take your details down, and the minute there is any kind of movement on the vehicle, I'll call you."

Claudia ended the call and looked at Jody.

"We're just going to have to wait this one out. I think you need to let your parents know. I doubt they'll want to speak to me right now."

"Sure," said Jody. "I'll head on over to their place now." She wiped a tear from her cheek and added, "You know what's funny?" she said, "Gareth reached out to Dad today, and you know what Dad said? He said he had to go to work and that he didn't have time to talk about things like divorce. After that, Gareth simply got into his car and left."

Claudia felt the hurt and anger from earlier welling up in her throat. She could imagine how Gareth must have been feeling when he got behind the wheel.

෴

"Claudia, there's a call for you," she heard one of her staff calling from the doorway that led to the office. "Should I take a message?"

Claudia lifted herself from the floor and straightened her pants, "I'll take it," she said, "Give me a second, and I'll be there."

She sat down at her desk, her legs shaking. She was terrified of every call that was going to come in from then onwards, but she knew she couldn't miss one of them. The call was transferred, and she stared at the receiver as the line rang its familiar ring.

"Hello, it's Claudia speaking," she heard herself say. "How can I help you?"

"Claudia?" she heard a man's voice on the other end of the phone. A client? She thought, wondering who it was.

"Claudia, it's Alex."

"Oh God, it's *you*," she whispered, overcome with a rush of exhilaration which quickly turned into guilt. She had no right to be on any emotional high under the circumstances. She had not heard his voice in seventeen years, but hearing it now sent quivers of prickling excitement down her spine.

"I've been so worried about you, Claudia. I wanted to make sure you were okay after what happened this morning. I know I'm taking a chance phoning you like this, but I've been going out of my mind. I had to reach you somehow."

Claudia smiled. "It's so strange to hear your voice after all this time, Alex. I just wish that it could have been under different circumstances."

She took a deep breath. "Alex, something strange has just happened. I can't tell you all the details right now, and I can't speak for long because I am expecting a call from Satnav."

"Satnav?" asked Alex.

"It's Gareth. He left the house a couple of hours ago. He was furious. He was threatening all sorts of things. He told me that I have blood on my hands, and now his car has disappeared off the radar."

She could hear Alex breathing down the phone. "Do you think he's going to do something stupid, Claudia?"

"God, Alex, I hope not. Personally, I don't think he would do anything to hurt himself. I'm hoping he's just trying to scare me. But when he spoke about me having blood on my hands..."

Alex sighed. "I haven't told you this before," he said, "but when Christine told me that she wanted a divorce, I went to a very dark place. I couldn't see how I could possibly continue my life without her in it. I started to think about ending my life. I went to the hardware and bought a hosepipe and duct tape. I kept it in the trunk of my car for weeks. I even researched how to "do it". I'd picture sitting in my car in the garage with the engine running and drifting off into a deep sleep as the carbon monoxide fumes filled my lungs."

Claudia sighed deeply.

"Alex, that's terrible."

"But I didn't have the balls to do it, Claudia," said Alex. "I honestly couldn't go through with it. One day, I hooked the whole contraption up, taped the hose pipe closed through the window, and was just about to close the driver's door and turn the key in the ignition when I saw my step-daughter walking down the passage towards the garage. That was my awakening, realising that she could have walked in there later and found me dead. I couldn't do that to her. So, I decided to get on with the business of living instead. Gareth will be fine, Claudia, you'll see. He probably just needs some time out to cool off."

Claudia smiled. "Thank you, Alex. I appreciate that, and I really hope you're right. Hopefully, Satnav will pick his car up on their radar soon."

"Chin up, girl," said Alex, "You'll hear from him soon. Just know I'm right here thinking about you, okay? Please message me if you need anything, even if it's just to talk."

"Okay," she said softly. "I will. I promise."

CHAPTER 7

Claudia sat at her desk, toggling through emails, trying to keep her focus off Gareth, but thoughts of where he was and his state of mind were all-consuming.

Jody had sent her a couple of text messages asking if Claudia had received any news, but the answer was always the same. There was no news. Claudia had also texted Alex, trying to keep him up to date, but as night fell, the situation seemed to become more and more hopeless.

The sun was setting, and her office was getting dark. She thought about serving dinner, but she felt sick to the stomach. She looked up as Kyle walked into the office.

"Mommy," he said. "There's a man at the gate, and it looks like one of those cars that the people at the hospitals drive with the red flashing lights. Can I let him in?"

Claudia felt her blood run cold. In her heart, she feared the worst but couldn't bring herself to even contemplate it being a reality.

"I'll let him in, my darling," she said as she stood up, putting an arm around her little boy's shoulders. "I wonder what he wants?"

"Maybe he knows where Daddy went. Maybe they found him," he said, smiling up at Claudia, taking her hand and leading her into the house.

Claudia pressed the gate control pad, and the gates swung open. She could see the swaying of the red and blue lights from behind the wall. She watched the paramedic walk towards the front door, and she prayed with all her heart that Gareth was okay.

He was a tall man, balding with wisps of brown hair emerging from the edges of his receding hairline and day-old stubble on his face.

"Good evening, Ma'am," he said. "Are you Mrs Stevenson?"

Claudia nodded, waiting for the words she hoped she didn't have to hear.

"Mrs Stevenson, I'm afraid there's been an accident. It involves your husband."

Claudia felt Kyle's fingers tighten in her hand.

"Mrs Stevenson, your husband has been in a serious car accident, and…," he lowered his voice, "and I'm so sorry, Ma'am, but your husband didn't make it."

"Oh my God," Claudia heard herself saying, her mind in a whirl. "*Oh my God!*"

She felt Kyle's fingers slip from her grasp as he ran and buried his face in a pillow on the couch, tears streaming from his eyes, sobs choking and engulfing him. Ross stood in the stairway, motionless.

"Mommy? Is Daddy coming home?"

"Oh my God," said Claudia again, falling to her knees. She wanted to cry out, more in anger than in anguish. Why was this happening to their family? Why did he have to die? Surely this was all a big mistake? This couldn't be real.

She looked up at the paramedic. "Are you sure?" she asked. "Are you sure it's him? Are you sure they've done everything they can to save him?"

"Ma'am, I've been on the scene for the past two hours. He hit a cement truck head-on. There is nothing left of his car. When I left the scene, the firemen were still there, trying to cut his body out of the wreckage. It's definitely your husband, ma'am."

He reached into his pocket and pulled out Gareth's identification book. It was covered in brown soil. There were burn holes on some of the pages. Claudia looked at his photo. She started wiping the soil off the cover. She could smell death – it rose off the pages like that sick black smoke that rises from a burned-out field. She felt the smoke grab hold of her hand and the life force draining out of her body. She wanted to vomit. She quickly closed the book.

"Does he have any other family?" the paramedic asked. "Parents? Brothers? Sisters? We need to tell them as soon as possible. Can you call them? Are they close enough to drive here?"

Claudia nodded. "Would you mind waiting here until they get here? I don't think that I will be able to break this news to them on my own."

Claudia walked over to her phone and dialled Gareth's parents' home number. The phone rang on the other side, and his father picked up.

"Dad," said Claudia, "I need you to come over to the house as quickly as you can. Something has happened to Gareth."

Gareth's father didn't ask any questions.

"We're on our way," he said, a sense of stilted emotion hanging in the air, and put the phone down.

Claudia and the children sat in silence as the paramedic walked back to his car to fetch something that he wanted to give to Kyle and Ross. Kyle's face was swollen from all the crying, and Ross was sobbing quietly, holding on to a Spiderman figurine that his father had bought for him recently.

The paramedic arrived back with two knitted teddy bears.

"Volunteers make them for us," he said. "We give them to children when they lose a parent in a situation like this."

He handed a teddy bear to each child.

Claudia stared blankly at her children, completely devoid of emotion, utter disbelief consuming every fibre of her being. She kept hearing what must have been Gareth's final words, repeating in her head: "I'll never take you back!"

And that song, that haunting song.

She heard footsteps coming through the front door and looked up. It was Gareth's parents.

"Where is Gareth?" she heard Gareth's mother ask. "Where is my son?"

The paramedic put his hand on her shoulder and said calmly. "Please come and sit down, ma'am. I need you to sit down for this."

Gareth's father stood motionless, refusing to sit down. Gareth's mother slowly lowered herself into a chair, clutching her handbag, her eyes wide, wanting to hear the words but not wanting to hear the words, the finality of the truth tightening like a noose around her neck.

Jody arrived, tears pouring down her face. She sat on the edge of her mother's chair and put her arm around her as the paramedic delivered his verdict, "He didn't make it, ma'am. I am so very sorry. We did everything we could, but there was nothing we could do to save him."

Gareth's mother shot up out of her chair before she had even begun to digest the words, hatred, loathing and anger rising off her skin as she moved towards Claudia.

"Murderer!" she screamed. "You murderer, you bitch, you fucking murderer!"

Claudia felt her head wrenched backwards as Gareth's mother grabbed hold of her hair in one hand, and a cold thud as Gareth's mother's fist ploughed into her face, over and over again. And then there was that warm, wet feeling as Gareth's mother spat in her face over and over again while she hit her, the words "murderer" raining down on her like shrapnel.

Claudia grabbed her head, feeling tufts of hair pull away in her hands, and buried her forehead in her lap, praying that the assault would stop.

"Look at her!" she heard Gareth's mother scream as she delivered another blow. "She won't even cry – she *can't* even cry! She's a murderer, a bloody fucking murderer!"

"Ma'am, if you don't stop this, I'm going to have to call the police," she heard the paramedic shouting over Gareth's mother's screams. "I think you need to leave now."

"Call the police!" Gareth's mother screamed out. "And make sure they arrest this bitch who murdered my son!"

Jody and her father quickly put their arms around Gareth's mother and moved her away from where Claudia sat, and steered her in the direction of the front door.

"You will pay for this, you bitch!" Gareth's mother shrieked as she was guided out of the house. "You will pay for this, you murderer! Stay away from this family, do you hear me? We don't want you at Gareth's funeral – you're not welcome there, you fucking bitch!"

Claudia could not move. Her legs felt like jelly. The room was silent as she heard their car start up outside, and she felt her ears ringing. Her head was throbbing as she wiped the saliva splats from her cheeks, the horror of what had just happened slowly sinking in. Kyle and Ross were holding each other tightly, their eyes wide with fear, clutching their knitted teddy bears. They had never seen this woman, their grandmother, the woman who had helped raise them from the day they were both born, behave in this manner. It was as if the Devil himself had taken possession of her.

"Ma'am, I would suggest that you lock your doors," said the paramedic in a firm but gentle voice. "That was not normal behaviour that I just witnessed, and I am scared for your safety. Would you like me to position a policeman outside your house tonight?"

Claudia looked up at him, embarrassed that he had been forced to watch that entire spectacle, wishing that this was a horrible nightmare and that soon she'd be waking up screaming, her pulse racing, but knowing that this was not real, that this was not happening in her life.

"We'll be okay," she said kindly. "I'm so sorry that you had to see all of that. Gareth and I had spoken about divorce this morning, so they are probably thinking that he wouldn't have died if things between us were better."

She showed the paramedic out, closed the gates, locked the front door, and walked towards the boys. She could smell the casserole still cooking in the slow cooker. She felt sick to her stomach, and she struggled to hold the vomit down. A feeling of dread came over her.

She had just killed her husband, and there was nothing she could do about it.

It was too damn late to fix anything now.

The boys were exhausted from crying and rigid from shock and fear. Daddy was gone, and the rest of his family had gone completely mad.

"Mommy," said Ross in a small voice. "Daddy forgot to take his suitcase with him. I'm sure he's coming back to fetch it."

Claudia hugged her children tightly. "I'm so sorry, my boys. I am so very sorry."

Claudia decided that Kyle and Ross would sleep with her in her bed that night. As she tucked them in, she shuddered with the thought that they were sleeping on their father's side of the bed, the spot where *he* should have been sleeping, not lying rigid and disfigured in a body bag in a cold, dark mortuary.

CHAPTER 8

Alex.

"Oh my God," she thought, "He doesn't even know."

She thought back to the last text message she had sent him, telling him how scared she was because there had been no news.

She wanted to phone him. To hear his voice. To hear him tell her that everything was going to be okay. She looked at her phone and keyed in his name. She hesitated, withdrew her hand and tightened her fist. She couldn't. She was afraid that she would crumble into a million pieces if she attempted to vocalise what had just transpired.

Claudia walked down to her office and opened her laptop. There was a message from Alex; he had desperately been trying to reach her.

August 22nd, 22:00 pm

Alex Winterton

My darling Claudia, please tell me that everything is okay and that you are okay!

I have been so worried about you tonight. I've been fearful to call you again just in case Gareth has returned. I didn't want to jeopardise anything you might be working on.

I desperately await your earliest reply.

And then another…

August 22nd, 22:44 pm

Alex Winterton

I guess you're not going to make it to our secret, secluded meeting spot here tonight. I waited for you, but I guess there are reasons why you didn't make it.

I honestly hope everything is alright and that Gareth is safe. I will be thinking of you the whole night as I try to sleep. I will look out for you early online.

Please, oh night, rush, rush, that thee might bring the morning light.

It was close to midnight. Her office was quiet except for the gentle humming of her laptop. She heard an owl hooting from the rooftop above her office and then a whoosh as it took off into the night, its powerful wings carrying it above the sad story that was unfolding in the house below it.

Claudia opened a new message in her inbox and typed Alex's email address. With her heart thumping in her chest, she told him the news…

Alex, Gareth is dead. It feels terrible to be typing these words. The paramedics came at about six thirty this evening. He hit a concrete truck head-on and died on impact. I don't know if this was planned or just a terrible accident.

God, Alex, they want me to identify his body tomorrow. I am absolutely terrified. I can't bear to see him like that. I'm not even ready to say goodbye.

I feel sick to my stomach, knowing that I was the catalyst for this happening.

His parents came over and physically assaulted me. They accused me of murdering their son. They don't even want me at his funeral.

Kyle and Ross are absolutely heartbroken. They cannot believe that their dad is gone.

I never thought that something like this would happen in my lifetime. It's as if everything has been suspended in time. I keep thinking that this is all a bad dream and that I'm going to wake up in a cold sweat, disorientated and dazed, but I would know that everything was okay. That the boys still had a father. That his parents still had their son.

But I know I can't. The nightmare has only just begun. I have so many people to answer to. There is so much to explain when I don't even know where to begin.

Alex, I am so sorry to have to tell you the news this way.

I promise to be in touch again as soon as I can.

Claudia closed her eyes and sighed, clicked the send button, watched the message leave her outbox, and then closed her laptop.

A cruel trick had been played, the wrong hand dealt, and the roulette wheel of her life began to spin out of control with greens and blacks and reds merging into a dizzying frenzy as the ball fell into its slot and the players waited on the side lines, holding their breath, hoping that their number had been chosen.

Alex had no idea that her world had shifted on its axis and that, once again, two roads had diverged in a wood, and a new path needed to be chosen. One where new relationships could be built and old ones healed. Where lives were to continue, albeit reshaped and remoulded after they were shattered and ripped apart.

When the sun rose the following morning, Alex opened his Inbox and felt his blood run cold as he read Claudia's message.

His hands shook uncontrollably as he typed his reply to her:

Oh my God, Claudia! I have no idea what to say to you or how you must be feeling right now. Please know whatever you might need, or however I might be able to help you, I am here for you at any time, day or night. Reply to me only when you are ready to.

Shrouded in a surreal cloak of numbness, Claudia stared at herself in the bathroom mirror. There were dark lines under her eyes, and it felt as if there was a ghost staring back at her. She felt hollow. Drained. Racked with guilt.

Claudia hurriedly dressed herself and left the boys sleeping in her bed, tiptoeing out of her bedroom and down to her office.

Claudia broke down in tears and crumpled to the floor as she told her staff the news. The look of disbelief on their faces quickly turned to tears. Nobody could have imagined that he was gone forever.

At that moment, Ross walked in, rubbing the sleep out of his eyes and asked in a tiny voice.

"Mommy, is Daddy coming home today?"

Claudia drew him close to her and sat him on her lap.

"No, my darling," she whispered quietly, "Daddy is in Heaven with the angels now."

She felt as if she was trapped between two worlds, and every fibre of her being was fighting to leave the dark world behind her.

Claudia could hardly believe her eyes when she looked up to see her father, who lived thirteen hours away, walking towards her. He had booked himself on to the first available flight from Cape Town to Johannesburg when he had heard the news. Claudia couldn't even remember telling him that Gareth was gone.

Her father smiled gently and put his arms around her, awkwardly wiping the tears from his eyes.

"I'm so sorry, my baby," he said. "I'm so sorry."

Claudia sobbed, "Dad, it's all my fault. I should never have asked him for a divorce. I should have never let him leave the house. I feel like I've stolen his life from him…"

"It's not your fault, baby," said her dad. "It's not your fault. You cannot blame yourself for this. I won't allow it. I'm going to help you get through this, and I don't care how long it takes."

Claudia looked up at her father and smiled.

"Thank you, Dad. I think you're going to be the one to put all the broken pieces back together."

Within a matter of hours, the house was buzzing with people. Some were weeping uncontrollably, but many stood quietly in small groups, talking in low voices, trying to understand why Fate had dealt such a cruel twist in this family's lives.

Grace came in carrying a few bags of shopping. She looked at Claudia and shook her head. Claudia vaguely remembered calling Grace the previous evening to tell her the news. Grace had winced, remembering the accident that she had driven past that evening on her way home. It was terrible. There was a truck lying on its side and a black Renault Cabriolet in pieces all over the road. Grace had turned her head away as she drove past, not realising that it was her friend's husband trapped in that car.

"I have no words, my friend," she sighed, wiping the tears from her eyes. "I just wish I knew what he'd been thinking. This is insane."

Claudia's father quickly busied himself by sorting through piles of paperwork and told Claudia that he was going to start the process of informing the relevant people of the death of his son-in-law.

"I think the first thing we need to do is get hold of his life insurance company. I'll do that if you can talk to his staff."

Gareth's staff, a crew of mostly Mozambican men, were milling around outside the house, unsure of whether they should head off to work their current building project or not, not quite comprehending that their "boss" was no more. Claudia's father had gone outside to have a word with them.

For Claudia, it all felt like too much. An entire family chain had been snapped in the middle, and it felt as if the pieces had been scattered so far and so wide that it was going to be impossible to bring them all back together again.

Claudia sat down and prepared Gareth's final wages for his staff, using, ironically, the money that Gareth had left the boys. It was blood money, she thought, and she was damned if she was going to watch the boys spend the cash on anything that could further tie them to the reminder of his words that day. She would rather use it to pay off his staff.

One by one, the men came through, and Claudia handed them each an envelope.

"I'm so sorry," she kept saying. "I'm so sorry."

Paulos, a gentle giant of a man with scars that told a thousand stories lining his face, put his dark hand on top of Claudia's and, in his broken English and a single tear furrowing down his cheekbone, said, "If there is anything you need me for Madam Claudia, please you know my number, I will be here. Boss Gareth did so much for me. I want to help you like he helped me."

Claudia's heart was breaking. Gareth was a good, kind man. He was loved by everyone. Why was he never able to see that in himself, she thought?

Kyle was having trouble breathing, and he was sobbing uncontrollably, his little face swollen from the tears.

God, Claudia thought, how was she going to keep this all together? She felt as if she was starting to fall apart, and watching Kyle, his perfect world completely shattered, unable to deal with the fact that his father had been wrenched from his life, was destroying her from the inside out.

One of her staff had made an appointment with her house doctor and ushered Claudia and Kyle into her car.

"You are both going to fall apart," she said soothingly. "Let's get you to the doctor and get you something to calm you down a bit."

The doctor prescribed tranquilisers and sleeping tablets, and Kyle's sobbing subsided as the medication slowly released itself into his system. No eleven-year-old should have to deal with such a tragedy, Claudia thought. This was so wrong on so many levels.

A policeman arrived at the house, and Claudia was asked to travel with him to the mortuary to identify Gareth's body.

"It's just part of the procedure, ma'am," the officer said as Claudia shook her head wildly.

"I can't!" said Claudia. "I can't bear to see him in that state. For God's sake, you *know* it was him in that car last night. Who else would it have been?"

She felt the nausea rising up in her throat. It was one thing to imagine how he had died and how he must have looked when the paramedics arrived on the scene, but it was another thing being required to see a corpse, a battered, disfigured body of a man who had loved and adored her, albeit somewhat warped in his final years, and she could not come to terms with the possibility of being haunted with that final memory of him. She was terrified that it might be the final nail in her mental coffin at that point, the final touch that would send her reeling over the edge and plummeting into a deep, dark mental abyss.

"I can't," she begged. "Please don't make me do this!"

She felt a hand on her shoulder and looked back to see Eric and his wife, Annie, standing behind her. They both loved Gareth, and there were lines of anguish all over their faces.

"I'm going to go down to the mortuary on your behalf, Claudia," said Eric warmly. "Let me handle this. It doesn't have to be you that identifies him."

Claudia hugged them both tightly.

"Thank you, Eric, I can't thank you enough."

"Alright, ma'am," said the police officer. "Once your husband's body has been identified, it will be sent to the coroner so that they can perform an autopsy. You will need to collect that report from us once it has been produced because there are people who will be looking for it – his life insurance company and the car insurance companies. The truck that he hit was also written off, so *their* insurers will also be looking for the full report."

Claudia suddenly realised that she hadn't even thought about the driver of the cement truck.

"Was the driver okay," she asked. "Was the driver of the truck okay?"

"He was very shaken, ma'am," said the police officer. "Your husband came out of nowhere. When the driver swerved to miss your husband, he was too late. He watched everything happen right in front of him. It happened so quickly, and on impact, the truck overturned and rolled down the embankment. But he's okay. He can't remember much. It is probably the shock. But there are other witness statements that we are working through, and I hope that through them, we can figure out what actually happened last night. I'm very sorry, ma'am."

Claudia walked back into the main living area of the house, where her father and some close friends were talking about the funeral arrangements. Claudia still had to get herself to the funeral parlour. Everything was happening so quickly. There was so much that needed to be done.

"Mommy," said Kyle. "Please can I say goodbye to Daddy at his funeral? I never really said goodbye to him. I want to stand up and tell everybody how much I loved him."

Everyone at the table put their hands out and touched the brave little boy. "Of course you can, my darling," said Claudia, smiling gently, "In fact,

I think that would be amazing. You will be the perfect person to tell everybody what a wonderful man your father was."

Was.

Gareth *was*.

That night, unable to eat the dinner her father had cooked for her, the nausea from the shock of her new reality consuming her body, Claudia opened her laptop and typed a note to Alex, knowing how worried he must be about her.

August 23rd, 19:40 pm

Claudia Stevenson

Alex, I just wanted to let you know that I'm okay.

My dad has flown up from Cape Town, and the house is filled with friends and people who care.

It's going to be crazy for a while. There is so much to do.

I promise to be in touch as soon as I can.

The following morning at breakfast, Claudia called her father away from the table and quietly mentioned that she had to go into town to meet with the funeral director. She would need to set a date for a funeral later in the week, and she desperately wanted to close this chapter of her life before it ate her alive.

Claudia got into her car and drove up the street. She waited momentarily at a traffic light, watching other people drive past, some looking ahead focussed on the road, others laughing and chatting to each other in the car, some swerving around each other. It's amazing, she thought, how life just carries on. Everyone, in some way, is fighting their own battle, dealing with their own lives, and in that moment, people would have looked at her and been completely unaware of what she and her family were going through.

Claudia wanted to get out of her car, put her hands in the air and scream out in pain, "Look at *me*! This is not a normal day for me! My husband has just died, and you're just driving around as if nothing has happened!"

She wondered how many other people were driving around in a similar zombie-like state as if their lives too had been frozen in time and they were waiting for somebody to hit the *play* button again.

The visit to the funeral parlour was draining. Surreal. Twenty-four hours earlier, Claudia could never have imagined that she would have been picking out a coffin for her husband, discussing the cremation arrangements and trying to remain mentally intact when she was told that an open casket in the church was not an option because Gareth's face and skull had been completely disfigured during the impact of the crash and that no mortician would be able to stitch his face back together in a way that would make his appearance acceptable to those who would see him.

The picture of Gareth in his final moments haunted her. The emotion, the anger, the truck, the sound of splintering glass and crunching metal, his face being ripped apart, his body being crushed as the car crumpled around him. And that final blow as his soul left this body, glass shards tinkling to the ground. And then the sound of hazard lights flicking as passers-by stopped at the scene of the accident to offer their help, the eerie sound of an ambulance in the distance, the absolute horror of it all.

Claudia nervously called Gareth's parents to tell them that she had started with the funeral preparations, but she was met with shouting and screaming on the other end of the telephone.

"I want my son back, you bitch!" Gareth's mother shrieked down the line. "You stole him from us, and now you're trying to cover it all up with a funeral!"

Claudia shook her head as the sound of the phone slamming down on the other end reverberated in her ear.

Alex had, in the meantime, been anxiously waiting for some form of contact from Claudia. He had been wanting to call her since he had replied to her message the day before, but he knew that he had to give her the space and time that she needed to deal with everything that was going on in her life right now.

August 24th, 21:24 pm

Alex Winterton

Dearest darling Claudia,

Writing to you is the only way that I can stop myself from going insane at the moment.

I am so glad that you have people around you who care for you and are with you. In that sense, you are truly blessed. I wish I could be with you over this time, as I want nothing more than to hear from you what is going on in your inner world.

How are the boys coping?

Claudia, I honestly couldn't believe what I was reading when I opened my mailbox yesterday. I went ice cold. I just sat there in a daze, reading and re-reading your message. I had no idea what to say to you because I knew that nothing I said could or would change anything.

The weirdest thing is that I had a really bad night's sleep the night Gareth died, and when I woke up the following morning, I couldn't shake the heaviness I was feeling. I felt your pain and anxiety but didn't know why. I wanted to message you that night to touch base with you and ask you how you were doing, but I wasn't sure if Gareth had returned, and I didn't want to complicate things by sending you any messages.

Then, yesterday morning, I received your message. You have no idea what it did to me. I was completely stunned. I had so much craziness running through my head, heart and soul. Thoughts between how you were feeling, how I had influenced this, his parents, your dad... so much craziness!

The entire day was a huge blur. Even now, as I write this, I feel numb.

Claudia, I truly need to know how you are feeling. I also know we need to connect – and hopefully sooner rather than later.

I also need to help you – in any way possible. Please just tell me what that might be. I hope that everything I am saying is making sense because I feel out of my body even as I type this to you.

I think I have put more than enough pressure on you for now. If you need to, just reach out, and I will be there.

Caring so deeply for my soulmate right now...

Claudia tossed and turned in her bed that night. Every time she closed her eyes, he was there in front of her. Gareth. And his family. Pointing their fingers at her. She longed for the peace of sleep to overtake her body and transport her away from everything.

She felt so selfish, wanting to put this chapter in her life behind her. She knew that Alex was in the wings waiting for her, but she also knew that she had a husband to put to rest and two grief-stricken children to comfort and guide through this tragedy. She felt completely inadequate, knowing that she was both the cause of their grief and yet also the only one who could help them.

More than anything, Claudia wanted to make some kind of sense of what happened. Gareth was not there to answer her questions, and she wanted so much to believe that this was all just a terrible accident and that nothing she could have done could have stopped him from dying that day.

She knew that her only option was to take one day at a time. Perhaps, in time, the answers would find their way to her.

Claudia lay in bed listening to the sound of her children breathing quietly in their sleep. She popped out a sleeping tablet, turned it over a few times in her fingertips, put it in her mouth and then swallowed it. She switched off her bedside lamp and watched as the patches of light and dark in the bedroom played tricks on her mind.

In a strange way, she almost expected Gareth to appear, hissing those words, "I'll never take you back!" as his dark shadow grew, its fingers snaking up from the floor to the ceiling, spreading out across the room like black ink – dark black blood – accidentally spilt, his eyes looking down on her, his mouth open and hollow.

Slowly and thankfully, she felt consciousness slipping away from her, taking her into the bliss of sleep where, for a few hours, the world as she knew it would cease to be.

CHAPTER 9

There was a message on Claudia's phone from the police station saying that Gareth's accident report was ready for collection. Although Claudia's father had offered to take her down to the station, she decided she wanted to do this on her own. She wanted to give herself space to take the information in, whatever that information might be.

The police officer, a woman, casually opened the folder in the presence of another officer while Claudia stood to one side. Claudia looked away as the other officer covered her mouth and hastily moved Claudia away from the contents of the folder.

"I'm sorry, ma'am," she said. "There's a photo from the accident that I don't think you should see."

"I know that his car was in a pretty bad state," said Claudia quickly. "You don't have to hide this information from me."

"It's not the car, ma'am," cautioned the police officer. "It's your husband. It was a picture of his face. It was how he was found."

Claudia felt her heart jump. "Oh God, no, no, I don't want to see that. Please just give me the report and let me leave. I don't need the photo."

"Of course, ma'am," said the officer. "Here, take it. There's a detailed report about the accident. I hope you find the answers you're looking for."

"Were you able to figure out what happened that night?" Claudia asked.

"It was inconclusive, ma'am," said the officer and sighed. "The road markings indicate that your husband swerved suddenly – perhaps to avoid something in the road – but before he could get back on to the other side of the road, the truck was there and... well... ma'am, it was just too late. But there are reports from witnesses saying that he was driving at over one hundred and sixty kilometres an hour when he swerved onto the other side of the road, so we don't know if he simply lost control of his car. The post-mortem report at the back will give you more information."

Claudia walked back to her car, holding the report in a large brown envelope.

She sat down in the driver's seat and slowly pulled the report out. There were diagrams and road markings showing the point of impact and a hand-scrawled description of what vehicle A had done and what vehicle B had done. Then there was the post-mortem report. Claudia slowly read the words.

Cause of Death:

Multiple injuries

EXTERNAL APPEARANCE OF BODY AND CONDITION OF LIMBS:

WHITE MAN SEEN WITH HEAD INJURIES

THERE ARE OPEN FRACTURES ON BOTH LOWER LEGS

THERE ARE EXTENSIVE SKULL FRACTURES WITH THE FACE AND HEAD FLATTENED

EXTENSIVE BRAIN DAMAGE

THE TONGUE PROTRUDES THROUGH THE MOUTH

Claudia felt herself gagging and quickly reached for the car door, retching and vomiting on the sand road of the parking lot. She could not read any more. The list went on and on, but she refused to allow her eyes to see any more words.

Gareth was merely a body with a body number, and she couldn't bear to think about him in the state described in the autopsy. She couldn't bear to think that he was like that because of her. Every fibre of her being was racked with guilt and horror. How was she ever going to make peace with herself?

Sobbing, Claudia returned home to find her father packing the car with baskets of food, pillows and blankets. He held his arms out to her as the tears streamed down her face.

"Dad, it's awful. I killed him. I did that to him. It's all my fault."

"I know how difficult that must have been for you, my baby," he said, brushing the tears away. "But I refuse to believe that this was your fault, and I won't let you believe that for one second either. I'm taking you and the boys out into the country for the day; you need to clear your mind."

He took the accident report from her hands and smiled gently at her.

"Try not to think about it too much now. There's nothing you can do to change what happened."

The guilt continued to eat away at her soul, festering like maggots on a carcass.

It was a beautiful day. Her father had driven them to a nature reserve. It was a place where he had taken Claudia and her brother during their early childhood. Everything had seemed so much bigger back then, Claudia thought. She remembered running naked over the rocks, swimming in the warm rock pools, and sliding down the river along the smooth rocks on her bottom. She was so innocent then. She had never shattered another life.

Later that evening, after Kyle and Ross were tucked up in her bed and her father was snoring peacefully on the couch, Claudia walked across to her office, desperate to connect with Alex.

August 26th, 20: 24 pm

Claudia Stevenson

Alex, I still feel so dreadful about everything. I'm trying to pick up the pieces and move forward, but it's so damn hard.

I collected Gareth's accident report from the police station this morning, and I cannot even begin to explain the horror that flooded me to the core when I read it. I don't think that those images will ever leave my mind. It's as if they weren't writing the report about the same person, as if it wasn't Gareth. I couldn't imagine him in the state they described him in when they found his body.

Kyle and Ross were better today. My dad took us out to a nature reserve, a place he took us to as children. It was beautiful – for all of us. The boys had such fun with their grandad. I laughed and felt normal again.

Gareth's funeral is on Wednesday, and after that, a new chapter in my life is going to open. It's going to begin with the words, "One day, a long, long time ago, a handsome man and a beautiful woman drove to meet each other after being apart for more years than they could possibly manage. With outstretched arms, they embraced, and cried, and hugged, and kissed, and thanked the Universe for bringing them together."

Two weeks ago, we were living separate lives. And look at where we are now. Do you have any idea of how surreal this all is?

I am counting the hours until I see you.

August 26th, 10:44 pm

Alex Winterton

My darling, my soul aches for you, knowing what you are dealing with at the moment.

Time is the greatest healer, and it's important that you know that you will find peace within yourself one day. In the meantime, please know that I am here for you in every way possible.

I am glad that you spent time away from everything today.

The strangest thing is that on the one side of our story, we are mourning the tragic loss of a human being – a husband, a father, a son, a friend – while on the other side, we are celebrating a new life and new love. I cannot get over the irony of it all. It is all incredibly intense, and I am experiencing so many emotions right now.

I cannot wait to see you.

The light on the narrator began to dim. The time had come to lift the curtain.

The main character entered from behind the wings.

"Dad," Claudia said, somewhat uneasily as she shuffled in her chair. "I know it's been a couple of days – and I really feel awful for not saying anything about this sooner – but I haven't been entirely honest with you. There is something I have not told you."

Claudia's father raised one of his eyebrows and smiled.

"Oh yes? And what would that be?"

Claudia opened her heart to her father, telling him about how Alex had reconnected with her, the bond that had formed between them, and the feelings. Oh God, the feelings. She told him about how Alex had made her reassess her life and its direction and that she had realised that she could no longer remain trapped in her marriage to Gareth. No matter what happened between her and Alex in the long term, she had decided that walking through that door into this new life was not just a way out – it was the *only* way out.

Claudia's father was beaming from ear to ear. "You go, girl," he said. "Go and be happy. And don't hold back."

Claudia felt as if she was having this conversation with an old friend, not her father. He had given her his blessing. She was free to spread her wings and take command of this new stage in her life.

He told her about a time in his life when he had been married to Claudia's birth mother. She had refused to admit that she was mentally ill, that the Huntington's Chorea that he had suspected she had inherited from her mother was beginning to consume her mind. She refused to see a doctor. In fact, according to Claudia's mother, it was everybody else who was going mad, not her.

His life was miserable, and he had craved happiness and, more importantly – normality – more than anything. He didn't know that there was a way out until he met Claudia's step mother, a beautiful, kind young woman who swept him off his feet in a way that he never dreamed possible.

Claudia remembered the day of the divorce so well. She had returned from school, and her mother was pacing the dining room of their house. She was smoking. Claudia had never seen her mother smoke. The irony of it was that back in those days, smoking was considered "cool", and Claudia had always felt side lined by her school friends because her mother didn't smoke. Not realising what was going on and despite the obvious distress that engulfed her mother, Claudia distinctly remembered quietly celebrating to herself that her mother was now like all the other mothers.

"Your father has left us," Claudia remembered her mother saying. "He's left us."

Claudia's father explained to Claudia how he had to experience pain and suffering before he could find – and appreciate – true happiness. He told Claudia that *her* suffering was now over, that she too could find her true happiness.

∽

It had been almost a week to the day. It was time to say goodbye. The funeral arrangements were almost complete.

Gareth's family, like a pendulum on a clock, had spent the past couple of days swinging from blame and hatred to peace and acceptance. And back again.

Claudia's father had insisted that Claudia find some common ground with her in-laws before the funeral. She could not bury her husband alone. She had to find closure somehow.

They had driven through to Gareth's parent's house, where they were welcomed – albeit not with open arms – to find the family in conversation with the minister who would be presiding over the funeral the following day.

Kyle and Ross sat down on the carpet in the middle of everyone. Gareth's mother had taken out some of Gareth's childhood toys, a packet of plastic army men that he had played with as a young boy, and the children set them up, ready to wage war against each other.

The symbolism of that moment was uncannily ironic.

The minister was acutely aware of the tension that existed between the two factions of the family, and in an attempt to diffuse it, asked that everyone stand and hold hands, put aside any negative feelings that they might have, and focus on the life that was lost and what Gareth would have wanted had he been there, standing in the shadows, watching what was going on.

Grief contorted the faces of those who stood there. Hands squeezed hands. Eyes locked, and knowing glances were exchanged. The absolute horror and tragedy of what had unfolded just a short week earlier enveloped the circle of broken souls.

"None of this makes any sense," Claudia said to Gareth's mother as she sobbed on the edge of the bed, the loss of her son too great for her soul to bear. "I know you blame me, and I accept that you hate me. I wish I could turn back the arms of the clock and take all this pain away, but you know I can't."

"Claudia," Gareth's mother whispered. "You have destroyed our family. You have taken my precious boy away from me. I don't think I will ever be able to forgive you."

His mother turned and looked out of the window.

"Please keep that lesbian lover of yours away from the funeral. I will kill her if I see her. I will keep the peace until the funeral is over, but after that, I don't ever want to see you again. Do you understand me?"

Claudia stood up and leaned against the doorway.

"I understand," she said. "I just wish you would believe me when I tell you that I never wanted this. This was not how I wanted Gareth's life to end."

∽

Claudia's childhood school friend Gillian had stopped by to visit that evening, and Claudia shared her deep secret. Gillian remembered Alex well; she had been Claudia's best friend throughout high school and, in an amusing way, had been Claudia's "gatekeeper" when it came to Alex. She, too, was astonished to learn of their reconnection.

Gillian had been very close to Gareth and had known him for as long as Claudia had. She had been Claudia's maid of honour at Claudia and Gareth's wedding. She had been there through the births of Kyle and Ross. She, too, had watched the marriage fall apart. And now she was here.

The two women sat together and watched the flames dancing in the fireplace, Gillian holding Claudia's hands in her lap, fighting back the tears.

"I'm so happy for you, my friend," she said, "but dear God, this feels like a movie playing out. I can't believe Gareth is gone. And I can't believe that he has opened up this new path for you. It feels somewhat fantastical. Shit like this doesn't happen in real life!"

Claudia smiled, "I know, my friend. Isn't this crazy?"

After Gillian had left, Claudia lay back in bed and closed her eyes. In a few hours, she was going to be burying her husband. She wondered if she would ever be able to put her own soul to rest.

CHAPTER 10

There were so many people at the funeral that there was not enough seating for everybody. People were crowded in the doorway to the entrance to the church. There were people standing and leaning up against the walls inside. Children were sitting on their parent's laps and on the floor.

The congregation of mourners stood. Voices shook as they sang.

"Morning has broken, like the first morning. Blackbird has spoken, like the first bird. Praise for the singing, Praise for the morning, Praise for them springing fresh from the world."

These were the words that were sung on their wedding day twelve years earlier. Claudia had chosen them as the opening hymn for Gareth's funeral. She couldn't quite explain why. Perhaps she was holding on to one last remnant of their life together. She didn't know.

Claudia sat close to her children in the packed church. She felt Ross squeeze her hand, and she smiled tenderly down at him. His eyes were bright with tears. Kyle was fumbling with the cards he had written his speech on. He looked so smart in his black suit. He was trying to sing the words of the hymn, but he was choking on the lines.

She stared blankly at the coffin, which had been placed just a few metres in front of her. Her blood ran cold, knowing that Gareth's body lay inside it; the body of a man who was once so full of life was now just a body, and nothing could bring him back.

The service was a blur. Gareth's older brother Andrew was the first to stand at the podium and deliver his obituary. He reminisced about their childhood memories and how much he was going to miss having Gareth in his life, and then, regaining his composure, he glared at Claudia and said bitterly, "Claudia, one thing you need to remember is that Gareth loved you *very* much."

Claudia swallowed hard. She knew where these words were coming from. They were words of anger, charged with blame. She felt so responsible for everything. She knew that Gareth would not be in that coffin had it not been for her.

Jody walked up to the podium to deliver her eulogy to her brother. But the emotions overcame her, and she broke down, sobbing, her chest heaving. People rushed to her side to help steady her on her feet and then quietly ushered her away.

And then it was Kyle's turn. The little man in a child's body. The church grew quiet as he stood there, his little hands shaking as he held his notes, the oversized jacket that cloaked his tiny frame. The minister lowered the microphone to Kyle's level so that he could speak directly into it.

"Good morning, everyone," he said quietly. "I'm Kyle Stevenson, and I am Gareth's oldest son. I decided to stand up here today and tell you all how much I loved my dad, firstly because he was such a special father, and secondly, because he needs to hear me say these words to him today."

Claudia's heart, although it was breaking, was also bursting with pride for this strong little boy who was so determined to tell the world what a wonderful man his father was.

Kyle turned his focus away from the people in the church and looked at his father's coffin.

"Daddy, when you fetched us from school last week, you said goodbye and left, but we didn't know that this would be our last goodbye. I didn't tell you how much I loved you. I don't know if you knew how much I appreciated everything you did for me. You taught me so much, Daddy. Whatever you felt like doing, you did it. There were no limits. You wanted me to experience everything, and I did. You taught me to love animals. Thank you for my iguanas, my marine fish and all the birds you put in our aviary. Thank you for my meerkats."

He turned to face the congregation again, tears brimming in his eyes, his voice shaking.

"Dad, I loved how you used to wrestle me on the bed. I never thought you wouldn't be here to do that with me again…"

Kyle choked and, in between the sobs, said, "Daddy, I'm going to miss you so much."

Claudia sobbed. Every other person in the church sobbed with him. The grief was too much to bear.

Gareth had been a boy scout as a teenager, and he and Claudia had become involved in the movement again a few years before, running their own pack of cubs every Friday evening. As the coffin was carried out into the sunlight, the mourners were greeted by hundreds of scouts from the region. One of the scoutmasters placed a scout flag and one of the scarves from the pack that Gareth and Claudia had headed up on top of the coffin.

All the scouts gave the scout salute.

The coffin was carefully loaded into the hearse, and at that moment, Jody threw herself on to the coffin, screaming out Gareth's name.

"I can't let you go, Gareth! I'm not ready to let you go!"

Claudia watched as Jody was pulled back from the coffin, still screaming, and closed her eyes, wishing that she could be removed from all this madness.

∞

There was an eerie silence in the car as Claudia drove home.

There was a reception after the funeral. Claudia could hardly remember the details. There were people everywhere. People hugging her. People handing her cards and gifts. There was a plant. Where did she put that plant, she thought? People saying how sorry they were. People asking questions. People trying to provide answers. People crying. So many people crying. Gareth's family.

His parents keeping their distance. The glares. It was all too much, and eventually, everything became a quiet humming blur.

Normality. Claudia craved it like the scorched earth craves the rain after the sun's unrelenting rays have retracted and the moon steps over the horizon to cast its gentle light over the desiccated land.

But it was over now. Claudia could take her first steps towards the door to her new life.

But was Alex going to be part of that journey? Claudia swallowed hard at the thought. He was still going through his divorce. These things take time. He had a multitude of feelings to assess. He was still living with his soon-to-be ex-wife. He, too, needed to start his new journey. The timing could not have been more synchronised.

Or was it?

Claudia sat with her family and friends around the kitchen table at home, knowing that it was only a matter of time before people started leaving. The strange thing about funerals is how people slowly fade into the background once they are over. They get back to the business of living.

Claudia wondered how Alex was feeling. The past couple of days had been all about her, and she knew that he, too, was battling his own inner demons. She hadn't had a chance to check her inbox before the funeral, although he *had* sent her a text message that morning wishing her good luck and sending her strength. It wasn't in his usual upbeat style. Claudia found her mind wandering to a barren land scattered with the carcasses of animals that had taken their final steps and collapsed to the ground, exhausted and hopeless. She stood alone, Ross on one side of her and Kyle on the other, with no compass to guide them on their way.

Claudia excused herself from the table and opened her laptop. There was a message from Alex.

August 29th, 13:15 pm

Alex Winterton

Hi there gorgeous,

As I am typing this, I am thinking about you, Kyle and Ross. I hope the funeral went smoothly. It is so important for you and the boys to begin your individual healing processes now. I know that this is not going to be an easy path.

I had a deep chat with a close friend of mine, Ryan, last night. As I mentioned to you before, you are the only person who knows about Christine and me and our divorce. He was sharing his business and relationship success stories with me, and he told me how everything he has been working on has paid off. Then he asked how I was doing. I kept tap-dancing around my relationship with Christine, focussing on business instead, all the while wondering when I should break the news to him. When I finally did, he went dead quiet, and I saw tears in his eyes. I saw a spiritual side to Ryan that I had almost forgotten he had. Although the alcohol was flowing and I could feel my body was (physically) drunk, my mind was sharp. We connected on such a deep level, and he promised me that, no matter what, he would be there for me.

This morning, I woke up in a peculiar place, not physically, but mentally. I was trying to figure out if it was the alcohol or just unresolved issues within myself. I think that there is a lot I still need to work through, and perhaps as 'happy' as I feel on the surface, I need to drill deeper.

Last night, while I was chatting with Ryan, I thought to myself that I could easily make the mistake of becoming a deep spiritual recluse, and as much as this might be important for my spiritual growth and development at the moment, I don't want to cut myself off from the rest of the world.

There is so much running around inside my head at the moment.

I am going to focus my attention on work for a while, and I will look out for you later. Let me know if you see me online. I'm not sure what your movements will be like later.

I look forward to hearing from you all about your day, what happened, and how you felt about everything as it unfolded.

I miss you and our conversations.

Claudia sat outside and reminisced about the day with her family. Gareth had been put to rest, and it was now time for everybody to pick up the pieces of their lives and move on.

Would she ever meet Alex in the flesh? She had an uneasy feeling that his sadness was an attempt to reassess his situation and that perhaps he was having second thoughts about taking the next big step with her. She could not bear the pain that flooded her body as she contemplated the thought that Gareth's death was in vain, that Alex had come into her life and ignited a spark that quickly spread out of control like a wildfire, consuming everything in its path, sending Gareth out on the road that night, placing that cement truck in his path, until it finally ran out of fuel, gasping for air, fading away, the last remaining flames flickering and leaping into the air, grabbing onto anything, everything, but nothing.

Just death.

The eerie silence of absolute destruction.

CHAPTER 11

"So, how did it go?" Denise asked.

When Claudia had warned Denise against coming to Gareth's funeral, Denise was devastated. She has as much of a right to be there as anyone else. How could they think that Claudia was leaving him for her? Nothing could have been further from the truth. Denise had moved on with her life months ago – there was no more "Denise and Claudia" – she had made that very clear to her friend.

But Gareth still had his suspicions. Why else would Claudia agree to a divorce? Gareth had been very vocal about Denise the morning of his death when he had driven through to his parents. Being extremely conservative, the idea of their daughter-in-law leaving their son to run off into a lesbian relationship pushed them far beyond their comfort zones. It was inconceivable – the ultimate betrayal.

"Denise, the funeral was so sad," said Claudia. "And I missed having you there. I'm so sorry that the family placed so much of the blame on you."

"I guess they just need *somebody* to blame," said Denise. "Sometimes it's easier to lay the blame at another person's feet rather than take any responsibility yourself."

"What do you mean?" asked Claudia

"Claudia, he reached out to his parents that morning, and they chose not to give him the support he needed. They could not have imagined that he would lose his mind the way he did that day. Just as you allowed Gareth to leave the house, not realising what his intentions were, so they did the same."

"Our number one responsibility as parents is to protect our children and keep them safe," Denise continued. "This was the one time that they couldn't – and didn't – and they didn't see any of what transpired that day coming. It's easier to blame *you,* and it's easier to blame *me* than to admit that they, too, played a role in his death – even though *he* made the decision to be reckless. Not you. Not me. Not them."

"This is just so bloody complicated, Denise," sighed Claudia. "Honestly, if I could just have Gareth back for half an hour, I would sit down with him and get a sense of what on Earth he was thinking that evening. I cannot believe that he was in a rational state of mind when he took to the wheel; surely he knew he was dancing with death when he drove at that speed, straight into oncoming traffic? Was he trying to make a point? Was he just trying to hurt himself? Was he trying to show me the lengths he was prepared to go to in order to make a point to me about how much I meant to him?"

Denise sighed on the other end of the telephone.

"This is beyond fucked up, my friend. Nobody will ever know. We will always be left guessing. I wish I had the answers. Claudia, I'm hurting too. I miss Gareth. He was such a huge part of my life. I am sorry that he walked in on us that night. I know how much it destroyed him. And then he still tried to make room for *me* in your relationship. He never once lashed out at me. I just wish that he had believed me when I told him that it was over between us."

"I know," said Claudia. "Me too."

"Claudia," said Denise cautiously, "I didn't tell you this, but when Gareth fetched the boys from school that day, he told me he was planning on taking them away from you."

"Taking them away from me?" Claudia asked, confused. "I don't understand."

"I saw him standing alone while I was waiting for the school bell to ring. I walked over to him and gave him a hug. He told me what had happened that morning, and we spoke about what was going to happen in the future. He was broken, my friend, broken. It was as if he wanted you to hurt as much as he was hurting. He told me that he was going to take everything from you, just like you had taken everything from him."

"Oh my God, why are you only telling me this now?" asked Claudia, trembling.

"I haven't had a moment to speak to you properly since Gareth died," said Denise. "I've been wanting to tell you what happened, but it's been so difficult, especially now that his parents are on a witch hunt for me."

"Shit."

"I'm sorry, Claudia."

"It's not your fault."

"I'm sorry."

"So what happened after he told you this?" Claudia asked.

"Well, I told him to calm down before he did anything stupid. I asked him where he was planning on taking the children."

"What did he say?"

"He said he wasn't sure. But that he was thinking about the holiday house."

"God," said Claudia. "He could have killed them too…"

"I know. My blood goes cold just thinking about it. I suggested that he take the boys home and use the time to cool off, speak to you, and work things out. But he had this look in his eyes that I couldn't quite make sense of. It was as if something or someone else had taken control of his mind. I was so scared, my friend, but in the end, I just hugged him and told him that everything was going to be okay."

Claudia sighed.

"And then he left with the children. That was the last time I saw him."

He had been flirting with death. Touching it. Teasing it. Luring it in and then pushing it away from him. It was over, but was it really over? Claudia shuddered at the thought of her children being in Gareth's car with him that afternoon. He must have been so damn angry. He was prepared to take everything down with him if necessary. Thank God *some* common sense had prevailed, and he had brought them home with him.

"What were you thinking, Gareth?" she asked out loud. "What the hell were you thinking?"

She felt a vibration. There was a message on her cell phone. It was from an unknown number.

"I'm thinking of you," it read, *"Be strong. I have been there myself."*

There had been so many messages over the past couple of days. Streams of words. Messages of sympathy and hope. There were no messages laced with judgement. And yet the guilt – the guilt over her role in his death – fed on her. It consumed her words. She was harbouring a secret that could topple everything if it was revealed. It was never supposed to be this way. She had simply agreed to a divorce, and divorce was supposed to take time. There would be counselling. There would be time for new lives to be established. New people would filter in and out. Alex would have filtered in at some point. Emotions would have been dealt with. Gareth would have found somebody else. The children would have alternated weekend visits with Claudia and Gareth.

Isn't that what everybody else did?

Why did her life have to be so different?

Claudia was aching to connect with Alex. She lay in bed that night, cuddling and talking to her boys. They still had so many questions. Ross wanted to know when he was going to "get a new dad". Kyle was more reserved; it hurt him too much to imagine his life without a father.

Would Alex be that new dad, Claudia wondered. She had pictured a new life with Alex without even considering that there was a possibility that they would meet and then realise that this had all been a terrible mistake, that he still loved his wife, that he wasn't ready to inherit another family and fill a gap left by another lover.

She tossed and turned in bed. When had she last slept through the night, she thought?

The school the boys attended had planned a prayer ceremony for that morning. Gareth was not the only parent who had passed away in recent weeks; four other parents at the school had suffered similar fates, all in the space of a month. Gareth was the fifth.

She walked down to the kitchen and switched the light on. Her laptop was on the kitchen table, and she sat down and watched the bright red embers of the coals in the fireplace as they held on to the heat contained within themselves, pulsating gently, drawing on each other for strength.

She opened her laptop and wrote to Alex.

August 30th, 3:25 am

Claudia Stevenson

I cannot sleep. It is so darn frustrating.

I have been thinking of you solidly for the past couple of hours, wondering if you are sleeping now, knowing that you will be getting out of bed soon. I am longing to see you, to touch you.

If only I could clear my mind, just for five minutes, so that I could fall asleep! I shall try, and if I don't, I will lie awake thinking of you, thinking of us, and thinking of the amazing future we are going to have together.

August 30th, 8:16 am

Alex Winterton

How do you do it? Not only do you write so well, but you touch every part of my existence when I read your messages.

I am about to get into the shower, and who knows, perhaps I'll find you there under the soap... nice thought (naughty grin).

P.S. I cannot wait a minute longer to see you. I know that it's just around the corner, but how do you feel about Sunday? I was thinking about a picnic out in the country. The place that your dad took you and the boys to sounded amazing.

Think about it and let me know...

The prayer ceremony was incredibly moving. One of the families had lost both their mother and their father in a motorbike accident. Another mother had lost her husband in a car accident as well, except that she had been in the car at the time with her three daughters. He had been the only one who didn't make it.

Tragedy. Somehow, it's different when you have no say in how it all ends – when it is just a freak accident. There would be no malice, no forethought, no advance planning, no lesbian love affairs and ex-boyfriends appearing out of the blue.

Claudia wondered how long it would be before the truth came out.

"How are you doing?" Claudia heard a woman's voice behind her and turned around. She didn't know the woman but realised that it was the woman who had also lost her husband in a car accident.

"Did you receive my text message?" she asked Claudia. "I sent you a few words of comfort because I know what it feels like to lose a husband so tragically. I had to reach out to you somehow."

Claudia smiled, remembering the text message she had received the day before. "Thank you," she said warmly. "I wasn't sure who it was from, but now I know." And then Claudia added, "I'm so sorry about your husband. I know you must be going through hell."

"Do you know what the worst part is?" said the woman, her eyes bright with tears, "I can still hear that *drip, drip, drip* sound. When we had the accident, I blacked out for a couple of minutes after the impact. When I woke up, our car was upside down, and I was hanging from my seatbelt. I remember checking on the girls in the back. They were unconscious, but they were breathing. They had their seatbelts on. But my husband didn't. His head was smashed against the windscreen, and there was blood everywhere. All I could hear was dripping. *Drip, drip, drip.* It was his blood. It was dripping from his head on to the dashboard. His skull had been ripped open. Parts of his brain were exposed. *Drip, drip, drip.* I can't get that sound out of my head."

Claudia shuddered and thought back to Gareth. She saw the words of the accident report in her mind. She felt the bile rising in her throat. She wished she could shake the guilt that consumed her. She felt so responsible – that she had pushed Gareth over the edge. That he was alone in his car that day, a man with no hope, his soul destroyed.

She felt so wretched and so goddamn empty. There was a sadness attached to this ending that no new beginning could ever erase.

CHAPTER 12

Gareth's brother Andrew was on his way to the house to collect some of Gareth's personal effects that he felt he and the family were entitled to. Claudia knew that it was going to be awkward, and she was dreading the thought of a fresh confrontation.

She felt her skin prickle as she watched Gareth's father, his brother and his wife walk down the driveway from her bedroom window.

The conversation was brusque as they moved through the house, removing animal trophies from the walls. Claudia had always hated them; Andrew was a hunter and had donated various artefacts to his brother over time. Gareth had also built an aviary a couple of years earlier where he had housed exotic birds. There had even been a pair of flamingos. The aviary's climate had been unsuitable for many of the birds, and Claudia's heart had broken each time another dead bird was discovered.

Much to Claudia's dismay, Gareth attempted to extend the longevity of these beautiful creatures and had taken – amongst other things – a crumpled flamingo and a beautiful yellow-billed hornbill to a local taxidermist and had their lifeless bodies with their vacant, glassy eyes stuffed and mounted on to wooden blocks and then on to various walls in the house.

Brightly coloured birds, a Kudu head, several Impala heads, and African masks. Claudia watched as they were carried out of the house. Suitcases of clothes. A zebra skin rug. They knew that she would never have held onto these items.

She understood that they wanted to hold on to as much of Gareth as they possibly could. Perhaps they felt that Gareth's things would be safer with them than with Claudia.

Before they left, Andrew asked Claudia not to cut Ross and Kyle off from the family. It felt strange for Claudia to be negotiating future visitation rights with a man who was once so close to her heart.

Gareth's family had demonised her, and she was terrified of what they would be capable of if they ever found out about her relationship with Alex.

She felt a ripple of sadness flow through her body. The life we live and those we live it with become our frames of reference, our filters. The identity formed by being part of another moulds us into who we are. But when a soul is extinguished, and its light goes out, where do those people who are left behind find their true north?

Living in the house where she and Gareth had built their lives together was becoming more unbearable with each passing day. The reminders were everywhere. Claudia had to leave. She was praying for the right buyer. Her business was still operating from the house, but she had recently purchased offices in an office park close by. Gareth had been putting the finishing touches on the building, and she was due to move in by January. But January was going to take too long, she thought. She could pack up and move the business there within the next couple of weeks. She would deal with the incomplete finishes.

She thought of their holiday house and the promise she and Gareth had made to the children that they would live out there one day. Even though they would no longer be able to build their dream house, there was no reason why she couldn't move out there with the children and start over. The holiday house was tiny, and Kyle and Ross would have to share a bedroom, but at least they would be far removed from the house where their lives were torn apart. Moving away from the memories felt like the right thing to do. She would enrol the children in a new school and spare them the constant reminders that they would receive from teachers and classmates of the personal tragedy that they so desperately needed to put behind them.

Fighting her own inner demons, Claudia just wanted to remove herself from everyone and everything that tied her to Gareth and his family. She wanted to glue the tear in her life's canvas and carefully paint over the damage. But deep in her heart, she knew that just as the eeriness of the house was creeping deeper and deeper under her skin, the memory of her past would continue to haunt her no matter how many fresh layers she tried to paint over the wound.

Gareth was busy with so many other building projects before he died, and Claudia's father felt that the honourable thing to do would be to visit each of Gareth's clients and tell them the news.

Claudia could not stop thinking about Gareth's business. He was so proud of his work, but at the same time, it brought him so much stress. He never seemed to be able to stay on top of things. Projects running late, over-demanding clients, cash flow problems… he had dug himself into a hole that he just couldn't pull himself out of. Every day, he got out of bed and went to war. It was no wonder he struggled to find inner peace.

Claudia often thought that it was his business that ultimately killed him. It sapped him of all his inner strength. Claudia's words were simply the final nail in the coffin.

And ironically, he now has the peace that he struggled for so long to find.

She wrote to Alex.

August 30th, 12:03 pm

Claudia Stevenson

Alex, Sunday sounds perfect. This feels surreal on the deepest level. I still cannot believe we're actually going to meet in the flesh.

Despite all the confusion and uncertainty that surrounds me at the moment, I feel as if I have been given a second chance, a chance to love again in a way I never dreamed possible.

I truly cannot wait to see you.

Hearing his voice on the telephone was one thing, but seeing him in the flesh was another. She longed to run her fingers across his face, through his hair, to feel herself enveloped in his arms, his body touching hers. The mere thought of it was tantalisingly unbearable.

But then there was the guilt. The absolute harrowing guilt. That Gareth had sacrificed himself like a lamb at the slaughter so that she could find true bliss.

Where was the sense in all of this? *Was* there supposed to be any sense? Was she losing her mind?

August 30th, 14:54 pm

Alex Winterton

Hello, my angel,

I get a sense that everything that is happening with Gareth's family is taking its toll on you. It must be difficult to express yourself fully in writing here, so I want you to share everything with me when we see each other on Sunday.

You have been wonderful for me today. Just knowing you are there, having you to lean on, to share my deepest fears with. The energy I feel is overwhelming.

Talking about divorce is one thing, but physically going ahead with it is another. My complacency has passed its sell-by date. It's time to pack my bags, gather up the things that are important to me, close the boot of my car, and drive away from this life. But it's harder than I thought it would be, Claudia. It's not easy to erase six years of marriage in the blink of an eye. But I know it's time, and I'm ready for it.

I am incredibly blessed to have you in my life in the way that I do. Be prepared to hear lots more about the way I feel about you in the days, weeks, months...and years...that lie ahead.

I keep having to pinch myself when I think about us and where we now find ourselves. Whoever would have thought that in three sleeps you were going to be whisked off by your prince to a secluded location for our reunion...

Alex had left the office late, dreading having to drive home and face his own reality. While he drove, he dialled Claudia's number, hungry for her voice, aching for their connection. He had driven around the block in his suburb several times before they had said their final goodbyes. Christine was probably home, and he did not want to raise any suspicions in terms of what he was up to.

Even though his circumstances were different, he still felt the need to be sensitive towards the needs of the woman that he had loved for so long.

Christine had been unfaithful to him on more than one occasion during their marriage, and he had begun to doubt himself both as a man and as a husband. His own fidelity had remained strong despite her numerous affairs, but for reasons that he could not explain, he did not want to hurt her by revealing this new love that he had stumbled upon.

Like a man thrashing his way through a thick forest, his skin torn and bleeding, lost, trapped and unsure of which direction to take, Alex found himself running and falling through the foliage that wrapped itself around the edge of the forest and out into the open, looking up into the cloudless sky, blinking, dazed, but certain that he was home.

August 30th, 22:43 pm

Alex Winterton

The time has finally arrived. Two soul mates are going to finally venture out of Cyberspace and meet each other in the real world.

Would they:

- *Make it to their destination without any physical interaction?*

- *Stop for a quick kiss?*

- *Rape each other?*

- *All of the above?*

His List:

- *Blanket*

- *Food (suggestions are always welcome)*

- *Wine*

Her List:

- *Her beautiful self*

- *Directions*

August 30th, 23:01 pm

Claudia Stevenson

Alex, do a quick reality check. Rewind to one month ago. I cannot imagine the forces that must have been at play to bring us to the point we find ourselves at now. It's quite incredible, actually.

I know that there is going to be no such thing as a quick kiss! I want it to be long and passionate. I want to breathe you in and melt into your arms. I want to be lost in time and space while our bodies and souls reconnect.

By the way, what do you think I should wear?

Claudia carefully typed out the directions to her holiday house, careful not to miss any important information.

As she hit *send,* she felt a shiver reverberate through her soul. She still found it hard to believe that this was all actually happening.

August 31st, 2:11 am

Alex Winterton

Do you know what? I am so very excited! Fuck!

Sorry for swearing in our secret garden, but I just can't believe this either.

I agree; let's not rush anything. I want to absorb every moment with you, from the moment I fetch you to when we finally lay down on our picnic blanket, and I can wrap you in my arms as we gaze up at the sky together.

Wear something white. I am picturing you in a long, white, flowing dress...

I really cannot wait, and I know that you feel the same way.

Sending you lots of kisses and dreaming of you in ways that you cannot imagine.

Goodnight, my angel.

CHAPTER 13

If an animal has been caged for long enough, it grows familiar with its surroundings and becomes trapped in complacency. It forgets that it ever wanted to be free. It no longer hungers for a life outside of captivity.

Presented with a taste of change, the animal might rear up and back into the corner of the cage, trembling with fear. With enough coaxing, it will edge itself forward, closer to the open door, carefully placing one leg in front of the other, shaking, sniffing the air, checking for threats that may lie in wait for it beyond the open door. It lets the fresh, new, unfamiliar air fill its lungs. It smells and tastes different somehow.

It is strange, but it is exhilarating.

It was dangerous territory that Alex and Claudia were venturing into, but they had each other, and that was all that really mattered.

August 31st, 7:45 am

Claudia Stevenson

Sunday is going to be incredible, Alex. It was so exciting planning our reunion together last night. I want this to be exactly as you have imagined it.

On a more sober note, I really admire you for your inner strength at the moment. You have so much still to go through, and it is going to take its toll on you in a big way. There might even be times when you might question whether you have made the right choice and whether it wouldn't just be easier to have let things stay as they were. Your productivity may slow down because of the emptiness that you may feel. As I have been told recently, it usually ends up getting harder before it gets easier.

It is important that you know that I am going to support you in every possible way through this, be it to take a load off, to share your tears, or to kiss you to sleep.

August 31st, 9:16 am

Alex Winterton

Claudia, what a wonderful message.

Your words about getting to a point where it gets harder and might be easier to stay the same are so profound. I say that because of something that happened this morning.

What I am about to say might sound strange (because it sounds strange to be typing it), but Christine came to me in tears. She was in obvious (emotional) pain and told me about a situation that she is working through with the new guy she is dating, and, believe it or not, I actually gave her advice on the situation and wished her well with where she is at.

Don't get me wrong, though, the experience was painful for me because I really do love her – honestly. She is a very special person, but she struggles *to see that side of herself. I feel sorry for her in a strange kind of way. I struggle to respond to her appropriately because she lacks self-esteem. The more I try to build her up, the less she believes me, and it just becomes a downward spiral of emotions.*

So there you have it. In my heart, I know that it's time to break free from this situation. I just didn't think that I'd find the whole process so confusing. I care for her deeply, and I want her to be happy. This is where it is important that I don't fall back into the trap of being sucked into her vortex because I fear that if I do, I may never get out again.

On a happier note, my heart and head are so crazy with thoughts of you at the moment. I find myself unable to wait for your replies to my messages. It makes me dizzy!

I was lying in bed this morning, and I found myself dreaming about caressing your body, my hands running up and down your silky skin. I was in quite a state by the time I got into the shower...

Just think, there are only two sleeps left and counting!

A million magnetic particles split in half and kept at a sufficiently long enough distance from each other would be no more aware of each other's existence than if they didn't exist at all. But a subtle shift of minute proportions could have these particles tumbling and falling towards each other, the earth-shaking with the impact of the passage, the force between the particles growing stronger and stronger the closer they got to each other until eventually they collide. Like two souls merging into one.

Claudia found it increasingly difficult to focus on the other areas of her life with anything more than punctuated distraction. What clothes would she wear? How would she style her hair? What perfume would she wear? Would Alex like what he saw? Would she be perfect enough for him? Would he see the things in her that Gareth had failed to see?

August 31st, 22:19 pm

Claudia Stevenson

Alex, what I am imagining is seeing you, running into your arms, and melting into you.

So, if I can get this right, I'm going to ask Gillian (who is staying over for the weekend) to drop me at a secluded spot to meet you before we drive off anywhere. It will have to be somewhere in the estate where our holiday house is, but not on the open road. That would be too impersonal. How does that sound?

Just make sure you've packed everything in your car the night before. I don't want to raise any suspicions with Christine – for your sake.

Hopefully, I'll see you online later. Otherwise, we will catch up tomorrow, my sweetheart, and then Sunday, our big day, eighteen years in the making.

September 1st, 8:45 am

Alex Winterton

Hello, you gorgeous thing.

I love your idea. I can imagine just holding you for hours and not even leaving from that spot.

A few things about this, though...

1. We would need to be very anti-social with Gillian. Would she simply drop you off and then leave?

2. How would I find this secluded spot?

3. I wouldn't want anyone you know from the estate to see us just yet – for your sake. We will have to be very careful.

I am shivering all over with total excitement.

You are so completely amazing. I cannot wait for the final piece of our puzzle to click into place.

Gillian had agreed to take Kyle and Ross out for the day, and Claudia was deeply grateful for Gillian's kindness. She wanted her day with Alex to be perfect from start to finish, but she was concerned about her children. It would be the first time that she would be spending time away from them since their father died, and it probably would not be the last.

Although Gillian couldn't wait to meet Alex again, she promised Claudia that she would drive her to their secret rendezvous spot and leave as soon as they knew Alex had arrived.

The excitement at being a part of this grand but somewhat surreptitious master plan sent a tingling thrill down Gillian's spine. She had to protect her friend from the neighbourhood's prying eyes at all costs. Kyle and Ross were to be shielded from this knowledge until the time was right to bring Alex out into the open. It felt perilous on one level yet exhilarating on another.

September 1st, 9:35 am

Claudia Stevenson

The plan is in motion...

I don't want anyone to see us besides us.

So here's what you are going to do...

When you drive in, drive down the main road. You will pass a complex of cluster houses on your left, and then you will reach a traffic circle with a wagon in the middle. Turn right at this traffic circle and drive down that road. The road will bend to the left. Just keep following it. You will see a beautiful forest on your right, and there will be a road on your right that winds through the forest. Turn and drive through the wooded area and over the bridge. Drive up the hill and turn right into the second cul-de-sac.

I will leave my yellow backpack on the corner of that road so that you know you're at the right place.

And that's where I will be, waiting for you.

Let me know with a missed call when you reach the main gate, and I will tell Gillian to leave me there and drive back to the house.

I feel like a naughty child. The thought of finally meeting you is completely exhilarating.

Claudia spent the day out on the water with Grace and Charlie. A series of new jetties had been built for the boats, and the first of September was the official launch day. At the clap of a gun, sixty-odd speedboats raced across the dam and back again. Claudia, Kyle, and Ross all screamed with excitement as Charlie navigated his boat over the wakes in an attempt to secure the lead.

It felt good to feel normal for a change.

Claudia couldn't help but find her mind drifting off in search of Alex, wondering how he was spending the day, wishing that time would hurry up so that they could be together at last.

September 1st, 10:01 am

Alex Winterton

Ah, girl, this is amazing. Now, I truly cannot wait.

I will look out for the yellow marker and the beautiful woman I will be embracing.

This is going to be fantastic!

September 1st, 12:06 pm

Alex Winterton

Logged in, but no one here, so I thought I would just say, "Hey girl, twenty hours and counting."

September 1st, 15:08 pm

Alex Winterton

Big sigh...

And here I thought I might find a message from you, but sadly, it's just me in here, all by myself, typing to you and counting down the hours to our secret rendezvous.

Seventeen hours and counting...

September 1st, 18:42 pm

Alex Winterton

Alas, no reply... Do you perhaps know who I have been thinking about all day?

Tomorrow has now totally consumed me. I can't think of anything else, and I can't wait to get to sleep later so that I can wake up first thing, get in my car and be with you.

Well, there you have it, fourteen and a half hours, and then we will be in each other's arms.

What a treat awaits us both.

Until later...

September 1st, 19:37 pm

Claudia Stevenson

Well, we're finally back at the house, and my dad has passed out on the couch (I think he had one too many beers today), Gillian is reading, the boys are playing, and I finally have you all to myself.

Sweetheart, you have taken over my head and my heart, and I cannot stop thinking about you, and especially tomorrow, and what is going to be thereafter. It was wonderful to sign on tonight and find all these beautiful messages from you. I just want to fast-forward time until tomorrow.

Tomorrow cannot come fast enough!

Eleven hours and counting...

I have no idea how I am going to be able to sleep tonight.

September 1st, 22:34 pm

Alex Winterton

Girl, my entire body is throbbing and aching.

I have pictured the following so many times today:

I'm driving to our secret spot, and I slow down as I see your yellow backpack on the side of the road. I stop, pick it up and place it in the trunk of my car.

Where are you, I wonder? And then I see you ahead in the distance, standing with your back to me (looking so goddam sexy). I quietly walk up to you, slide my arms around your waist, and press all of me against you. You collapse into my grasp.

I tell you not to turn around.

I slowly kiss your neck, and as I do, your head softly tilts to the side...

My girl, I am missing you so much right now, as I have been the entire day.

I am so looking forward to our special time tomorrow.

I really want you to sleep well tonight. Lie down and close your eyes, thinking all the beautiful thoughts you can of us, and I promise you, you will drop soundly off to sleep.

Thank you so much once again for being you and allowing me to share in your amazingness. I will thank you even more tomorrow.

Only nine and a half hours to go. Can you believe it?

Until the morning light, then...

Claudia read his message and shivered with excitement.

A Skype notification popped up on her screen.

Alex was online...

Claudia: *Are you there, Alex?*

Alex: *I'm right here.*

Alex: *I miss you!*

Claudia: *I miss you.*

Claudia: *Would you like tomorrow to be just as you imagined?*

Alex: *Totally.*

Claudia: *I keep reading and re-reading your words. Wow.*

Alex: *I kept thinking back to how I used to meet you each day at school.*

Alex: *...thinking that tomorrow is going to be so incredible.*

Alex: *Different to all those years ago, but at the same time, familiar.*

Claudia: *I like that. Familiar.*

Claudia: *I am so looking forward to tomorrow! I cannot wait to be with you after all this time.*

Claudia: *The angels have been watching out for the two of us!*

Alex: *...and they are very proud of their work right now.*

Alex: *I can't tell you how I am feeling right now.*

Alex: *I have been thinking about you and us SO MUCH today.*

Alex: *The whole day, in fact...*

Claudia: *And what were you thinking?*

Alex: *I will share it all with you when I see you.*

Claudia: *I wish you were here with me right now, my baby.*

Alex: *I do, too.*

Alex: *It is so amazing how close we have grown in just a month. And how it has intensified this last week.*

Claudia: *I know, although I have always felt so close to you, even with the seventeen-year separation.*

Alex: *In fact, I was thinking about that as well today. How we needed a seventeen-year break from each other. To discover and find ourselves. So that we could reunite on a completely different level.*

Claudia: *This is so deep, and you are so right.*

Alex: *It's beyond deep, Claudia. Today has been a build-up for me to this very point. And now I have the fortune of sharing this with you.*

Claudia: *I never thought I would find you like this.*

Alex: *It was divine timing.*

Claudia: *It really blows my mind, Alex. You have no idea. I thought I was going to be unhappy forever until you came along. We must be the luckiest people in the world!*

Alex: *In the Universe!*

Alex: *We have drawn each other back into our lives. In fact, we were always there. Just minutes from each other. We were continually circling each other until the timing was right for our worlds to collide.*

Alex: *Everything we have done from our first encounter, right up until tomorrow. Bit by bit, we have been circling closer and closer. And tomorrow, we collide in the physical world. What an emotional explosion that is going to be...Claudia, you truly bring out the best in me. Do you know this?*

Claudia: *I do, and you do the same to me...*

Alex: *Thank you! It's incredible how there is all this intensity between us, and we haven't even touched each other yet.*

Claudia: *I know!*

Alex: *That's why I have always said that we have to let everything unfold naturally. We cannot rush what the Universe has so kindly planned for us.*

Alex: *I was scanning through your Facebook profile today. It's my way of being close to you.*

Claudia: *I do the same. And I read and re-read all our messages.*

Alex: *You know what was so amazing for me last night?*

Claudia: *Tell me.*

Alex: *As you know, I always want to be truthful with you, and I have so much that I still want to share with you. But do you know what? There is more than enough time for us to do everything we want to and say everything we want to say.*

Claudia: *I know. Whoever would have thought? That I would be a part of you and you a part of me...*

Claudia: *Soulmates.*

Alex: *For sure. Soulmates.*

Claudia: *I just knew in my heart that there was something bigger at play when we found each other again. As you said earlier, we had to circle around each other and grow as human beings, go through all the hard stuff, before we could find each other as refined and beautiful souls.*

Claudia: *Do you realise that there are less than nine hours left before I get to touch you, feel you, breathe you?*

Alex: *I was just thinking that if we weren't careful, I could say to you, "Okay, I'm leaving to come through to you right now!"*

Claudia: *I couldn't think of anything nicer. But I must admit, I am loving this build-up! I think I am going to try your relaxation idea right now and try to get some sleep. So, my sweet love, I bid you goodnight until we meet tomorrow.*

Alex: *I am looking forward to the same.*

Alex: *Here's a big kiss...*

Claudia: *And here are one hundred more...*

Alex: *I look forward to seeing my image of our first moments together become a reality...*

Alex: *Second cul-de-sac?*

Claudia: *That's right!*

Alex: *Yellow back pack?*

Claudia: *Oh yes, it's packed and ready.*

Alex: *And a sexy girl at the end of the road?*

Claudia: *She'll be there.*

Alex: *I'm in heaven.*

Claudia: *Me too!*

Alex: *Log off and log in to Dreamland now, my love...*

Alex: *And I will see you there, I promise.*

Alex: *Eight hours and fifteen minutes...*

Claudia: *...and counting.*

Alex: *I am kissing your sexy eyelids right now...*

Alex: *Ready, set, go!*

Claudia: *Until tomorrow....*

Claudia lay back in bed and closed her eyes. She reached out and switched off her bedside lamp.

She took a deep breath in and slowly exhaled, allowing her mind to wander forward in time, trying to imagine what it would be like to feel his lips against hers, his soft breath on her skin...

CHAPTER 14

Time. Tick tock. Tick tock. The pendulum swung in a steady beat from right to left and left to right. Tick tock. Tick tock.

Click. The hour hand moved position. Years had become weeks, and weeks had become days. And now, as the pendulum swung back and forth, the days had become hours. Soon, it would be minutes and then seconds. And Alex would be there, standing right in front of her. Seconds would become milliseconds, and the pendulum would stop, and for a short while, time would stand still.

It was 5 am. Claudia opened her eyes, and she felt her heart skip a beat. It was Sunday. She breathed in deeply and smiled.

She thought about Gareth. The man who no longer lay beside her in her bed. The space was empty now. She closed her eyes and quietly sent him a prayer.

"Gareth, please forgive me... please understand that I never wanted to lose you like this... please forgive me for what I am about to do today..."

She looked up and grinned as she saw Gillian standing in the doorway.

"Good morning, lover girl," she said and laughed, bouncing down onto the bed and putting her arms around Claudia. "Excited?"

"You have no idea. I can hardly breathe."

"Three hours, and he's all yours."

"God. Please pinch me. I think my head is about to explode!"

Gillian rolled over and pinned Claudia down on the bed, pinching her all over.

"Wake up, Claudia, wake up, things don't get much more real than this!"

Claudia giggled and wriggled out of her friend's grasp, panting for air. "Okay, okay, I believe you! Honestly, I am screaming inside with excitement!"

Gillian lay on her back with her feet up against the headboard and smiled at Claudia. Claudia sighed as a tear rolled down her cheek.

"Are you okay?" Gillian asked, sitting up straight and putting her hand on Claudia's shoulder.

"Yeah, I'm okay. Just a bit overwhelmed, I guess. On the one hand, I cannot wait to see Alex, while on the other, I hope Gareth is oblivious to what is about to happen, wherever he may be right now."

"You've got to put this behind you, Claudia," said Gillian. "You're going to wreck this second chance at happiness if you choose to stay trapped in the past with all the pain and all the guilt. Gareth is gone now. Let him go. He's at peace now, and that's all that matters."

Claudia wiped the tears away and sighed. "I know. Logically, that would be the right thing to do –

just let him go and move on. It's just that everything happened so quickly. I'm scared because this all feels so goddamn right, and I keep thinking, what's the hitch? I don't deserve this. Not after what I did."

Gillian put her arms around her friend and squeezed her tight.

"Nobody deserves to have gone through what you went through, Claudia. And nobody deserves a bit of happiness more than you do. Now, come and sit outside with me and watch the sun rise on this beautiful new day. Grab a blanket, and I will make you a cup of tea."

"Thank you, my friend," said Claudia and smiled warmly. "You're such a special friend. Thank you for putting everything back into perspective."

The two women sat outside on the veranda and watched the sun peep over the horizon, spreading her fingers over the mountains and stroking the landscape awake with the warmth of her touch.

It was a new day, and a new chapter was being written.

∞

Alex quietly closed his car door and reversed out of the garage, careful not to wake anybody. His heart was thumping with excitement. The drive ahead was long, but as the distance spread out before him, he knew he was finally leaving his old life behind him. He watched the sun rising behind him and pushed down hard on the accelerator.

"Here I go," he thought. "This is it... "

"Where are you going today, Mom?" Kyle asked as Claudia buttered a slice of toast for him.

Claudia hated herself for the double life she was living, and she dreaded having to lie to her children, but she couldn't possibly expect them to grasp, let alone understand, what she was about to do.

"There are a few things that I need to sort out at home, my boy," she said, ruffling his hair, "but

Grandad and Gillian will be looking after the two of you today to make sure you stay out of mischief."

"Well, actually," she heard Gillian say from the bedroom, "We've got some mischief of our own planned for you and Ross today. Your grandad and I are taking you out quad biking for the day. How does that sound?"

Kyle's face lit up, and there was a squeal of excitement from Ross as he came running in from outside.

"When are we going? When are we going?" they asked in unison.

Claudia laughed as she cut the slice of toast in half and handed it to Kyle.

"You're going to have a great time today, my darling, and I'm going to miss you like crazy!"

Claudia smiled at herself in the mirror as she prepared the final finishing touches. She was wearing the white dress that Alex had hoped she'd wear.

She wanted to look perfect for him. She wanted to take his breath away. She wanted to be everything he had hoped for and more.

Her phone was ringing. She looked down at the number. It was Alex.

"Alex?"

"Good morning, gorgeous. I hope you're ready."

"I am," she said, smiling like a little girl. "Are you close yet?"

"I will be there in ten minutes, my darling."

"Oh God. This is so exciting!"

"I know. I cannot get to you fast enough."

"Well, hurry up, I'm about to explode with excitement," she grinned.

"I'll see you soon," said Alex. "Very soon. Now, get yourself over to our meeting spot. I cannot wait to wrap my arms around you!"

Claudia squealed as she ended the call and gathered up the pillows and her yellow backpack, packing them both carefully in Gillian's car.

"You ready for this?" Gillian asked, winking.

"I've been waiting for this my whole life," Claudia whispered, returning the wink. "Now, let's go!"

As they were driving down the road, Claudia's phone rang again. It was the control room at the main gate.

"Mrs Stevenson, there's a gentleman by the name of Alex Winterton here to see you. Can I grant him access?"

Claudia drummed her feet against the floor of the car, mouthing the words "He's here!" to Gillian as she turned the car and drove through the forest.

"Yes, yes, of course, yes, please let him in," said Claudia, suddenly nervous.

"Oh my God, Gillian! Shit! This is all really happening!"

Gillian laughed and accelerated as she drove up the road.

"Is this the cul-de-sac over here?" she asked, pointing towards the road on her right.

"Yes, this is it," said Claudia, somewhat breathless.

Gillian slowed down and popped the trunk open. Claudia opened the car door, stepped out and grabbed the yellow backpack, her marker.

"Okay. This is it!" she said as she closed the car door, "Thank you, my friend!"

"Now, don't go and do anything I wouldn't do," teased Gillian as she waved out of the window and drove off down the road.

"Well, I guess that leaves my options wide open then," laughed Claudia, waving back.

Claudia swallowed hard. She carefully placed the yellow backpack on the sidewalk and glanced down the road. Not wanting him to find her standing there, she walked quickly down to the end of the road, the leaves crunching beneath her feet as she entered the clearing. She walked under the trees and stopped, her breathing fast and her pulse thumping in her throat. She was waiting for him with her back to him, just as he had requested.

She turned around to see if she could see him and then suddenly she heard the sound of a car's engine. She caught sight of the black bumper and quickly turned back around.

She heard the engine switch off and the sound of a car door closing. She knew that Alex had picked up her yellow backpack and that it was safely in his car.

She was desperately trying to control her breathing, and it felt as if her heart was about to jump out of her throat.

She could hear his footsteps. One, two, three, four, five... she kept counting. She could hear his footsteps as they drew closer to her. Crunch... he was in the clearing, metres away from her. She wanted to swing around to see him but knew that she had to hold on for just a few more moments. The magic of the moment was tantalising.

The footsteps slowed down as they crunched through the leaves. And then they stopped. She could feel the heat of his body. He was right behind her. She felt as if she was going to collapse. She felt his arms weaving around her waist. She felt his breath against her skin as he kissed her neck, tilting it to one side, her body trembling.

"Can I turn around now?" she whispered.

She felt his hands on her shoulders and the slight pressure as he turned her body to face him. And there he was. Her boy. Her man. Her soul mate. He looked like an angel, the sun catching his long hair as a gentle breeze lifted it from his shoulders. Claudia looked up into his eyes, those kind, gentle blue eyes that she remembered so well, and she sighed, and they both smiled at each other.

"Hello, my darling," he whispered as he cupped his hands under her chin and brought his lips close to hers. Claudia stood up on her tiptoes to reach him. Their lips touched, and for a moment, the world span out of control. With their bodies pressed up against each other, their breathing almost out of control, they embraced and kissed, and suddenly, they were both laughing and crying.

The pendulum had stopped. There in the clearing under the trees. This was their moment in time where nothing else and nobody else mattered.

"I can't believe that we're here, like this, at last," whispered Claudia as she ran her finger down his cheek, wiping away his tears. "The circle is finally complete."

Alex grinned at her and kissed her forehead. "The best part is that this all feels so damn right!"

He took her hand and led her out of the clearing, "So, my gorgeous girl, are you ready to go on an adventure?"

"Hell yes!" laughed Claudia as she ran ahead of him, pulling him along. "I've been ready for weeks!"

She slid into the passenger seat and watched him get in. He was wearing white Bermuda shorts and a light pink shirt. Damn, he looked good, she thought to herself. She let her gaze flow over his body. He was perfect in every way. He was so much more than she had expected. She felt his hand run from her knee and up her thigh, and her whole body trembled.

Driving past the control room and out of the main gate, Claudia breathed a sigh of relief, knowing that nobody had seen them. She had to be careful to avoid rumours spreading should any suspicions be aroused. Kyle and Ross needed to be protected from this at all costs.

"So, here we are," said Alex as he winked at her. "It's just you and me and the open road."

He slowed down on the side of the highway to let the roof of his cabriolet down, turned the volume of the music up, and Claudia laughed and pumped her fist in the air in time to the drumbeat as they drove. For the first time in a long time, it was as if the rest of the world did not exist. An eraser had swept across the pencil drawing of their lives and taken away the fine lines of pain, the trauma, the hurt and the memories of their "other" lives that neither wanted to think about.

They parked in a secluded area in the nature reserve and made their way down to a section of the ravine where nobody would find them. They spread the blanket out under a tree, close to a rocky outcrop, with the sound of bubbling water rising up to meet them from the valley below. It was perfect. A cloudless sky, a beautiful setting.

Claudia lay back in Alex's arms as they watched the sky above them, running her fingers down his chest.

Alex turned and kissed her gently and then more passionately.

"Girl, you are so beautiful," he whispered as he touched her face, kissing her eyelids, her nose, her forehead, and then her lips. Claudia felt her fingers unbuttoning his shirt, exposing his skin. She kissed his neck and ran her lips across his nipples. Moving lower, she allowed her tongue to swirl around his belly button. Looking up at him while he stroked her hair, she grinned as she tugged on his shorts with her teeth, teasing him. She could feel him throbbing beneath her hands, and she giggled as she straddled him. He ran his hands down her breasts and gently lifted her dress over her head, his body aching for hers as he touched her skin.

She lowered her face to his, and they melted into each other, moving in unison, both wanting more. Alex slipped off her bra and ran his hands around her naked breasts.

"Hello!" they heard a voice calling. "Hello! Hello over there!"

"Holy shit!" whispered Claudia. "Shit, shit, shit!" There were two game rangers on the other side of the ravine – and a dog. "We've got company!"

Claudia quickly slipped her bra back on and pulled her dress over her head, cringing with embarrassment as she slipped off Alex. Alex was giggling as he straightened his shorts and buttoned his shirt, "You're lucky this pair has a tight zipper. This could have been a lot worse," he said, tickling her.

"Hello!" Alex shouted back at the voyeurs.

"Everything okay over there?" one of the rangers shouted back, "You're not supposed to be down there, you know. It's off-limits!"

"We're on our way out now," Alex shouted back as he helped Claudia to her feet. "There's a lot more about us that is off-limits at the moment," he whispered to Claudia and winked naughtily. "If only they knew."

"Oh Alex, can you believe it," laughed Claudia as they made their way along the ledge towards the rangers. "It's been nearly eighteen years of not being caught, and we've been caught *again*!"

Alex squeezed her hand. "And we can add *game rangers* to the list of people who have caught us in the act!"

After apologising profusely to the rangers for trespassing and hoping that they hadn't seen too much from where they had been standing, Alex and Claudia were released back into a safer, more communal area of the reserve, where they decided to unpack their picnic and enjoy their last few hours together.

"Claudia," said Alex, taking her hand and looking into her eyes. "There's something that I have carried with me since we broke up all those years ago. I need to share some information with you so that I can unburden my soul completely with you."

Claudia felt her heart sinking, unsure of what it was that he wanted to tell her.

"Okay, but you're scaring me right now."

"Don't be afraid. I am only speaking my truth."

He reached into his back pocket and pulled out a small white envelope. He handed it to Claudia. "Open it," he said.

Claudia opened the envelope and found a photo inside. It was Alex. On a beach. There was a huge heart that had been drawn in the sand in front of him, and he was on his haunches next to it. She looked closer, and there in the sand was her name.

She smiled. "Ah, Alex, I love this! Where was this taken? I've never seen this photo before."

"Claudia, remember when we went quiet with each other – when things just stopped working between us?"

Claudia nodded.

Alex sighed. "Well, it was our winter school vacation, and I went down to the coast with some friends. You couldn't come down with me because you were working during the holidays to save up for your university fees."

"I remember that," said Claudia, thinking back to that time in her life. It wasn't long after that holiday that he stopped talking to her.

"I was missing you so much that day, so I drew a huge heart in the sand and wrote your name inside it and asked my friend to take a picture of me next to it so that I could give the photo to you when I returned – that way you would know how much I missed you."

Claudia smiled and ran a finger across the photo.

"But something happened that night. I had a few drinks, and I met another girl. We ended up on the beach together, and I kissed her. It never went any further than that, but Claudia, when I realised that I had crossed the line and betrayed you, I could not live with myself."

Claudia looked up at Alex. "So you couldn't face me after that?"

"I couldn't even face myself, Claudia."

"Oh, Alex. Everything makes so much sense now. I could never understand why there was this distance between us. I felt hurt and betrayed, but I didn't know what I had done. I questioned everything about myself. I even asked myself if you were looking for more in me than I had to offer, knowing that I couldn't go back on the promise I made to myself. I thought you had lost interest in us. That's why I decided to break up with you."

Alex pulled Claudia towards him and embraced her. "I knew I was hurting you, but I believed in my heart that I would have hurt you more by telling you that I had betrayed you. It was easier for me to just detach myself from you, even though it was killing me."

Claudia shook her head. "I wish you had just told me, Alex. I would have understood."

"I just want you to know how sorry I am, Claudia. I have carried this inside me like a trapped bird for so long. I really am so sorry."

Claudia giggled and punched him playfully in the ribs. "Alex, let this poor bird free. I don't want you to have to carry that with you anymore. All that matters right now is that we have each other. The past can stay right where it is: in the past."

As each unburdened their soul, Claudia felt the connection between her and Alex strengthening. Alex felt it, too. The chemistry was electric on all levels. As he drove her home later that evening, Claudia's hair blowing in the wind and Andrea Bocelli's voice filling the car, Claudia rested her head on Alex's shoulder. She looked up at him and smiled.

"Thank you, Alex. For everything."

Alex leaned over, kissed her forehead and squeezed her hand. He was dreading the moment when he would have to say goodbye to her.

CHAPTER 15

There are many ways of living. Some people simply exist. They wake up every morning, slip out of bed, churn through their daily routines with very little sense of purpose, return to bed, and then repeat the whole cycle again the next day. And then one day, they slip away in the night, and the world carries on without them in it, and soon they are forgotten because, in reality, they left very little behind to remember them by.

And then there are those that choose to live. Really live. They may have simply *existed* at one point in their lives, but through a series of (often mysterious and sometimes heartbreaking and tragic) circumstances, something snaps inside. A seed begins to germinate, and life bursts out from inside, reaching up towards the sun, unfurling and drawing in the light, excited to make an impact on the world. That is living.

Claudia and Alex were acutely aware of the shift that was taking place in their worlds since they collided in the physical realm. Despite the mountain of challenges that lay ahead of both of them, knowing that they had each other made each step seem a little more surmountable.

Alex had returned home that night to find Christine pacing the house, demanding that he tell her where he had been, and finally walking out and slamming the door behind her when he refused. She was in a dark place, but Alex could not allow her to destroy his joy, not this time. He had spent years feeling as if he was treading in quicksand, certain that at any moment he would sink deeper and choke as the mud filled his lungs until there was only blackness – but now he felt an incredible sense of inner strength. His love for Claudia was his lifeline, and it was pulling him out of his quagmire of self-doubt and loathing. The menacing grey clouds were making way for the sun's golden rays to stream through. He felt alive again.

There was a message from Claudia that awaited him, and he smiled to himself as he lay in bed, alone but not lonely, isolated but not abandoned, and read her words.

September 3rd, 4:46 am

Claudia Stevenson

My gorgeous, amazing, super-sexy real-life soul-mate!

I cannot get yesterday out of my mind. It was everything I had hoped for and so much more. You're just as incredible in the flesh as you are in cyberspace. To say I had fun is an understatement. From getting caught half naked in the bush to the beautiful picnic where we said all those things that would have otherwise remained unsaid to driving home with the wind in our hair and a song in our hearts. If this is just a taste of our future together...

I feel like the luckiest girl in the world. Thank you for turning my life around.

I am going to spend the rest of my life thanking you.

Claudia had returned home to excited stories from Kyle and Ross as they stumbled over each other's words, re-enacting the day's events with Gillian and their Grandad.

"We had so much fun, Mommy!" said Kyle. "We went through streams and up the side of the mountain, and Grandad got stuck in a hole, and we all had to help pull the quad bike out."

Claudia laughed as she ran the bath. "And now it's time to scrub all of that mud off of your bodies."

Ross squealed as Claudia lowered him into the bath, Kyle splashing the water beside him and throwing handfuls of foam from the bubble bath at his brother.

Things were far from normal, but she savoured these little moments of normality.

"I love you, my boys," said Claudia tenderly as she tucked them into bed that night. "I really love you both so much."

∾

September 3rd, 22:17 pm

Alex Winterton

My dearest darling Claudia,

What amazing words, and how the thoughts come rushing back to me. From driving through the gates of your estate to hearing your voice over the telephone, to driving past Gillian and having her lean out of the window to tell me how excited you were, and then finally going on a hunt to find you.

And when I finally did, what a discovery. There she was, my angel from Cyberspace, manifested into living flesh and looking so gorgeous. The emotions and feelings that were rushing through my body and soul when I wrapped my arms around you are indescribable.

Kissing you as you turned and then looking into your beautiful eyes...

Our drive into the country, the lookout points, and finally finding our secret garden where we were allowed to play for a few precious hours before we were once again living up to our history of getting caught.

Then finally, settling down to rest with a beautiful spread, each opening our souls to one another.

Then, as you said, our beautiful drive home, holding tightly onto each other.

You turned a dream into a reality. Nothing more could I have ever hoped for.

I send these words to you with so much love, and I look forward to looking upon your beautiful face again soon.

Claudia smiled as she read his words. All the doubt and worry that had once consumed her drifted away like the seeds of a dandelion. She thought back to Gareth, her denial and shock and anger having dissipated to a state of acceptance, where she knew that her life had shifted one hundred and eighty degrees on its axis and that it was never going to turn back on itself again.

Gareth was really gone.

But she was still here.

And so was everybody else.

By moving on so quickly, by starting to live again and feel happiness again, was she betraying Gareth? Was she betraying Kyle and Ross? Were it not for Alex, she would be an emotional wreck – that much she knew – and she had to be strong for her children. She knew that as their mother, she was their only beacon of hope right now.

Claudia wondered if Gareth was watching her, sitting on a chair in the corner, shaking his head in confusion, tears rolling down his cheeks as he realised that he would never see his children again, knowing that it was too late to turn back the clock.

Because now he was gone. He was, as with so many people who once simply existed, nothing more than a memory of a life cut short.

Claudia stood, once again, at the edge of the cliff. She stretched her arms out and reached for the sky. She was falling, not to her death, but into love. She had never felt so alive. The extremes of her path and Gareth's were wild and abandoned and, in their disparity, so very, very sad.

September 3rd, 23:16 pm

Claudia Stevenson

My sweet angel, reading your words tonight has all but mirrored how I feel right now!

Seeing your car out of the corner of my eye and hearing your footsteps behind me... all I wanted to do was turn around and leap into your arms.

Feeling your arms around my waist, your breath on my neck. Asking you if I could turn around to see you, and when I finally did, knowing that my life had come full circle. Feeling your soft lips against mine, my heart almost stopping in my chest. Standing on my tiptoes to reach you.

The ease with which we closed seventeen years of being apart reminded me once more that you were always the one.

I read an article on soulmates today and thought I would share a piece of it with you:

"With soulmates, there is an instant knowing, an instant fit, an instant bonding. Soulmates could be

separated in a room of five thousand people, but if the time is right for them to come together, they will. When they look into each other's eyes, they do not see eyes – they see each other's soul. They have come back together from other lifetimes together to take their love to a higher level."

Never in my wildest dreams did I think that I would ever deserve a second chance at love like the one I have found with you. We are both so blessed, and I feel eternally grateful to the Universe for bringing you back into my life.

For me, there are no more questions.

September 3rd, 22:24 pm

Alex Winterton

My darling,

How unbelievably true are these words? Every time I looked into your eyes yesterday that is exactly what I saw: your beautiful soul and the story that it brings with it.

We have fun, we are connected, and we can just be with each other. I am living from the heart with you, and I honestly believe that it is way more than love that we have between us. I guess that's why it is strange for me to put a handle on my feelings.

Thank you so much for this, and yes, you are correct: no more questions.

I am dreaming of you, and I haven't even put my head down to rest.

Sleep tight, my angel.

Claudia undressed and smiled as she turned on the shower. The house was quiet, and she was alone with her thoughts.

It had been an emotionally taxing day. She had visited four of Gareth's clients with her father. The reactions had been interesting, ranging from disbelief and "If there's anything we can do…" to "Look, I can appreciate that he is gone and there is nothing you can do about it, but he took a fairly large cash deposit from us, and we're going to need to get that money back. Who is managing his estate?"

Claudia knew that there was no money left to give back. Gareth's debts were skyrocketing by the day. It's funny, Claudia thought, that in the end, once the emotions have settled, it all came down to money. Everybody wanted a piece of the pie.

I guess that's what everybody wanted while he was alive, she thought out loud, remembering how the financial strain took its toll on him on a daily basis. He was always spending more than he was making, and his financial woes were a vicious circle that spent most of their time spinning wildly out of control.

She stepped out of the shower, wrapping a fluffy white towel around her body and hugging it tightly against her skin. She wished that Alex was there right now, her beacon of light in the storm. How she wished that she could fast forward time and put all of this mayhem and uncertainty behind her. Gareth's past was haunting her as much as it had haunted him.

Claudia tossed and turned in bed that night as she thought back on the past tumultuous couple of weeks, wondering if she would ever be able to put that part of her life behind her. She needed to consolidate everything in her mind somehow. She thought about it and sat up in bed. Perhaps she could find closure this way. Perhaps if she wrote it all down it would ease some of the guilt that was clinging to her, refusing to let go.

She started to type.

When she was done, she took a deep breath and let herself weep. She sobbed for everything she had lost and all that she had gained. She grieved for Gareth, and she felt his pain tearing through her soul. The tears flowed for her children, her precious babies who had lost the guiding hand of their father so soon in their tender, young lives. She wept for Gareth's family, knowing that, for them, the healing process would be eternal and that they would struggle to find answers. Because there were no answers. There would only ever be questions. There would only ever be a hundred thousand whys.

And most of all, she wept for her salvation.

CHAPTER 16

Claudia's father had returned home, and Kyle and Ross had gone back to school. Claudia had begun the arduous process of packing her life into boxes in preparation for her move out to the holiday house with the children.

The weeks ahead became a series of secret, stolen moments for Claudia and Alex while their normal lives played out in the background, and those stolen moments were fraught with tension, the fear that they might be discovered and that the news would travel back to Gareth's family, Alex's wife and most importantly, Claudia's children.

For Claudia, it was an inner battle of two beasts. One was starving and undernourished, its hackles raised in fear, the anticipation of danger lurking around every corner. The other was tame and friendly, filled with serenity and compassion, born of trust and hope.

How she longed to feed the beast of serenity without the snarling, fearful beast knocking on her door.

It was the morning of the seventh of September, Alex's birthday, and they had decided to spend the morning together away from prying eyes. It was during the week, and Claudia knew that it would be quiet out at her holiday home with most of the weekend residents having returned to their homes in the city. She and Alex would be safe for a couple of hours. She would drop the boys off at school and then meet Alex at her new, unoccupied offices close by, from where they would drive through to her holiday home together.

She woke that morning to a message from Alex, who was already waiting for her at her offices two hours before she was even due to arrive.

Claudia smiled as she read his words…

September 7th, 6:20 am

Alex Winterton

Good morning, gorgeous girl,

It is 05h03 as I write this to you, and guess where I am? I am waiting for you outside your offices. I am watching the sky change colour as the sun rises over the horizon, and I am reminded of you and me: Just as the sun is dawning on a new day, so a new era is dawning in our lives now that we have each other. What an amazing thought!

My darling Claudia, I truly love you so much.

As I sit here, I listen to every vehicle as it turns the corner, longing for you to arrive.

I know that the day that lies ahead of us is going to be incredible, and I cannot wait to hold you in my arms and kiss you.

I love you, my angel.

Claudia could hardly wait, either. Every moment spent in Alex's arms was one step away from the insanity of the rest of her life. Bits and pieces of her past and her present lay stacked carelessly on top of each other, and, like a game of Jenga, Claudia knew that it would just take one uncalculated move to bring her carefully constructed secret crashing down in pieces around her.

She waved goodbye to Kyle and Ross as they walked through the gates of their school.

"See you later, alligator!" shouted Ross and grinned.

"See you soon, big baboon," said Claudia, laughing.

How she loved those boys, she thought as she drove down the road. Her sweet, precious boys. They were blissfully unaware of the double life their mother was living.

༄

Her heart skipped a bit, and her pulse started to race as she drove up to the empty office park.

There he was.

Her lighthouse. Her beacon of hope.

"Happy birthday, sweetheart," said Claudia as she locked her car and put her arms around Alex. "And thank you for the message you left me this morning. I can't keep up with you!"

Alex grinned and kissed her, and she felt herself melting into him.

"Let's get out of here," he said.

Alex parked his car behind the house, respecting Claudia's wishes to be cautious as she could never be completely sure of who might see them. They closed the curtains and lay down on the bed, sipping champagne and catching up on the week's events, holding each other, touching each other, both secretly aching to make love to each other for the first time but knowing that there was no need to rush something so beautiful, that the perfect place and the perfect time would present itself in time.

Life felt so normal when they were together. It was just so sad that they had to hide their love for each other from the world. But there were eyes. It was a close community, and people *were* watching. Opinions were being formulated, and questions were being asked.

Claudia's heart ached as she kissed Alex goodbye and got into her car later that day. He was returning to his life, and she to hers. His "other" family was waiting for him, and Christine and his stepdaughters had made plans for him that night. Just like Claudia, his secret life had been hidden from his family, and he was waiting for the right moment to tell Christine that he was ready to set himself free.

Claudia arrived home with Ross and Kyle, both eager to share the day's events with their mother, and gasped in shock as she looked into the near-empty koi pond at their front door. Fish were writhing about in a horrid state of hypoxia, and several were flapping about on the rocks, dehydrated and close to death.

"Oh God!" she thought, realising that she had neglected to take up Gareth's duties since he had been gone, one of those duties being to fill the koi ponds up with water.

"Gareth, how did you fill the pond?" she asked, wanting to sob out of sheer frustration as she tried to stretch the pipe towards the pond. *Damn it*, she thought, the hose pipe was too short. It would never reach the pond.

Eventually, she resorted to filling buckets with water and running backwards and forwards, pouring water over the beautiful white and orange fish, praying that they would not die.

She walked around to the back of the house and looked at the swimming pool. It was green, and algae draped itself down the sides of the walls. Claudia sighed, feeling helpless and hopeless. She had held herself together for the past couple of weeks, but now she felt as if she was losing control. It was a strange sensation that she felt; her head was fuzzy, and she could feel a part of her sanity slipping away from her. Was Gareth coming back to haunt her, she wondered? How much did he know?

She sat down next to the swimming pool with her head in her hands and let the frustration flood through her body.

"Are you okay, Mom?" Kyle asked as Claudia wiped away the tears.

"Oh my boy, I'm so sorry, your mother is just having a wobbly."

"What happened, Mom?"

"I'm just being silly. I don't know how Dad used to fill the pond with water. I don't know how to backwash the pool, and I can't find the chemicals. I feel so stupid."

"You're not stupid, Mom. You're just good at other stuff."

Claudia smiled. "Yeah, I guess."

Kyle put his arms around her, and Claudia hugged him close to her.

"We'll figure this stuff out together, Mom," he said warmly. "I can be the man in the house until you find someone to take Dad's place."

Claudia shuddered, his comment cutting close to her heart.

"Let's go and pack a few more boxes, my boy," she said. "Maybe we can move out to the dam before the end of next week."

"Cool!" said Kyle, smiling.

Claudia hugged him tight and laughed. "Come on then, scallywag, let's get this show on the road."

As she put her head on her pillow that night, she thought of Alex and how he was spending the rest of his birthday. She felt the tears welling up inside her. How she wished that their forever had officially begun and that the waiting game she was playing was nothing more than a distant memory.

༄

Alex called her the next morning and told her how Christine had blindfolded him and, together with his stepdaughters, had driven him to a surprise birthday party that she had put together for him.

It would probably be the last birthday she would be celebrating with him. Christine had to save face, knowing that nobody knew what was going on between them – that she was moving on.

Alex laughed as Christine removed the blindfold to the whoops of "Surprise!" from everyone in the room. All his close friends were there, and he spent the remainder of the evening enjoying the finale of what had already been an incredible day.

"Are you okay, my darling?" Alex asked, sensing her quietness on the other end of the line.

"Not really, Alex. I hit a bit of a wobbly yesterday."

"How so?"

"Well," she said, sighing deeply into the telephone. "My life has been a series of extremes since we reconnected, and yesterday was just another one of them. It was so sad to drive away from you. My heart aches more and more each time I have to do it. It's like I'm on this high from being with you, but then there's this terrible low knowing that you are going. I just can't explain it. So, when we said our goodbyes yesterday, I had such mixed emotions. I know in my heart that we need this time to pick up the pieces in our 'other' lives so that when we are finally together, we can do so without fear of being cornered by something or someone from the past. I must admit, though, that I am finding it very difficult to do this and would, if I could, gladly fast forward the clock to six months from now."

Alex sighed on the other end of the line. "Keep going, Claudia," he said. "I want to hear everything you have to say."

"So here I am thinking that I've got to get a grip and stop trying to control things, and then I arrive home and realise that the koi pond is pretty much empty, the poor fish are all half dead, and I have no clue how to get water in there. The taps are miles away. There is an irrigation point close by, but I have no clue how to switch the water on. I can plug the hose into the attachment, and then?! Things that Gareth used to handle are now suddenly my responsibility completely. So, small things like ponds that I don't know how to fill up, pools that I don't know how to backwash, light bulbs that I don't know how to change because they are too high up, children that want more of me than I am able to give right now, guilt over calls from friends not returned, I guess it was all just a build-up of stuff, and I suddenly felt so overwhelmed."

"Ah, my girl," said Alex. "I'm feeling your pain and frustration so deeply right now. First things first, all you need is an expert to show you how to do the things you need to do. I'm sure that if you have the right person showing you, you'll quickly have it figured out. I wish I could be there to do these things for you. It's just a pity that the timing is a little out at the moment."

"You're right, Alex," said Claudia and smiled. "I guess I'm just not used to having to do everything myself. Everything has been a shared responsibility for the past twelve years."

"I can't even begin to imagine how this is making you feel," he said softly.

"Alex, I know that the things I need to do are things that I can learn. In my frustration, I hadn't even thought of asking a professional, and I feel so silly for overlooking the obvious! That will be the first call I make on Monday morning."

"There we go," said Alex. "That's the girl I know!"

"And as for us, my darling," Alex continued, "I feel the same. I, too, wish that we were months ahead of where we are now. But we're not, and all we can do in the meantime is suck the juice out of the precious moments that we are given to spend with each other until the day comes that we can put all of this behind us."

Claudia nodded and smiled. "I know, Alex, and everything you're saying makes perfect sense. I know I need to be patient. Logically, this is so clear to me. But my heart is on its own mission."

"I hear you, my darling. Believe me when I say that," said Alex warmly. "We are both going to find ourselves encountering difficult and challenging times in the weeks and months that lie ahead, and we just need to both be there for each other. Everything will unfold exactly as the Universe intended. You need to believe that with all your heart."

"I love you, Alex," Claudia said as she lay back against the pillows, sighing deeply. "You're so good for me. You build me up when all I've been used to is being broken down. You give me strength rather than pointing out my weaknesses. You are just such a beautiful person, and I really cannot wait to be sharing every waking moment with you. I cannot wait to be able to wake up and see you sleeping peacefully next to me. To feel such love for a human being is so awe-inspiring."

Alex smiled as he listened to her words. "I love you too, my special girl. And I thank the Universe every day for bringing you into my life. We are so good together."

Claudia kissed the boys goodnight and lay down on her bed. She could see the full moon outside her bedroom window, and the sky was bright with stars. She thought about Alex and his outlook on life. She thought about herself and how her mind had become overgrown with the weeds of disappointment in the years she spent with Gareth as he sank deeper and deeper into his downward spiral of self-depreciation, pulling her down with him.

She knew that she had to get in there, like a trained gardener would, and pull out all the weeds. She knew that despite her own self-doubt, it would not be as difficult as she had imagined to clean up the mess, but that it was going to take time for her to re-educate her thought processes and see the goodness around her.

She thought about Alex's words – that they were "good for each other" – and she realised how right he was, that sometimes their heads would lead them off in the wrong direction, forcing them to analyse everything too much, so much so that they might end up lost and confused and not knowing which way to go.

But then, between each other, they would put the other one back on track.

❧

When Claudia arrived back at the dam that Friday, she found an envelope slipped under her door. She picked it up and carefully opened it. It was a handwritten letter from John, who lived over the road from her. He was not a weekender like many of the other people who lived out there. Instead, he lived there with his wife on a permanent basis. Claudia had developed a soft spot for him over the years and had enjoyed his company and his sense of humour. John had been very close to Gareth, and the two men had spent many evenings sitting outside on the patio, sharing their stories over a bottle of whiskey.

Claudia had never asked what they had spoken about, but she was glad that Gareth had somebody with whom he could unburden his soul, somebody who, unlike her, could see things from a different perspective.

Her blood ran cold as she read the words of John's letter. He had seen her with Alex. And not just once but many times. He was shocked that she had moved on so quickly and was questioning her integrity as a human being. He wanted her to know that what she was doing was horribly wrong and that she needed to rethink her actions before they blew up in her face.

Claudia sat down and folded the letter closed, carefully placing it back inside the envelope. Her heart was beating in her throat, and her legs felt weak. She looked out of her front door and saw the lights on behind the blinds in their kitchen. She swallowed hard. She had to set the record straight.

"Kyle! Ross! Would you mind if I popped over to chat to John quickly?"

Ross popped his head around the corner and grinned. "You can if you let us play PlayStation," he bargained.

Claudia ruffled his hair. "The house is all yours. I won't be long."

She picked up the letter and walked over to John's house. She knocked on the front door.

"Claudia!" said his wife Noreen warmly as she opened the door and saw Claudia standing there. "What are you doing here so late? Are you alright?"

"I am, thanks, Noreen, but if you don't mind, could I have a few minutes with John?"

Noreen ushered Claudia through the house to the outside veranda where John was sitting, tending the evening's barbeque.

He looked up at Claudia in surprise.

"John," said Claudia, showing him the letter in her hand. "Please can we talk about this letter?"

"Sure," he said. "Sit down."

"John, I know what this must look like to you, and I know that Gareth had a very special place in your heart, which makes this doubly difficult to talk about, but I need to clear the air with you."

John sat up in his chair and folded his arms. "Go on," he said cautiously.

"John, as human beings, we tend to show only one side of our lives to the outside world. The side of Gareth and I that you saw was not the side that was going on behind closed doors."

John shuffled in his chair.

"You must understand that our marriage was on the rocks, not just for a short period of time, but for the longest time ever. We naively thought that we could save our marriage by moving out here, but if anything, the move put more distance between us. On the morning of the day he died, we decided to end our marriage. It was difficult for both of us, but it was necessary. There was too much heartache between us and too many irreconcilable differences. I thought we could just go our separate ways like other couples do when they get divorced. Not for one second did I think that he would die that day."

"Claudia," said John, "your husband was a very depressed man. I picked it up on that many times when we spoke to each other. He never complained about you, but he felt as if his life was one continuous roller coaster. His business was eating away at him, heart and soul."

Claudia winced. "I know."

John continued. "One night, he sat with me and told me that sometimes he felt so down in the dumps that he wanted to get into his car and drive away from it all, but something he said to me that night really disturbed me. He said to me that if things got really bad and if he happened to be out on the road and saw a truck on the other side of the road, he would use it to take his life. He would smash into it as hard as he could and make sure it finished him off properly."

Claudia gasped. "Oh God no, John, please don't say that, please don't tell me his death was premeditated!"

"Claudia, I honestly believe that it was. When I heard how he died, I thought back to that conversation, and I knew that he had finally followed through."

Claudia felt the tears welling up in her eyes.

"I had my doubts, John," she said. "I wanted to believe that this was all a horrible accident, that Gareth was in the wrong place at the wrong time, but the way things unfolded that day has made me question his motives over and over again."

"Claudia, it was no accident. I can promise you that," John said and sighed as he stoked the coals in the fireplace. "What *has* confused me is seeing you with another man so soon after Gareth's death. It opened up even more questions for me. I don't want to sound crass, but have you no respect for your husband?"

"Oh, John," said Claudia, wiping the tears away. "This other man is not just 'another man'. He is someone I reconnected with while Gareth and I were going through a particularly bad patch a couple of months ago. We know each other from our school days – we had been high school sweethearts – and he found me online. There were never any plans to meet in the flesh. We both respected each other's lives. We both knew that being together would never happen. He knew about Gareth, and I knew about his broken marriage, but that was it."

John scratched his chin. "So when Gareth died, you decided to take a leap of faith?"

"We did," said Claudia. "But we had no idea that the connection between us was going to be as strong as it was. I have never felt this way about anyone before. I know that this is right. I cannot explain how or why, but I feel it in my soul."

John smiled. "I was shocked when I saw his car parked outside your house and how you had closed the front door and the curtains. I have always been so used to everything being open when you were home. I knew you were hiding something when I saw you trying to cover your tracks and maintain a low profile."

Claudia sat back in her chair and sighed. "I'm sorry, John. I know what this must have looked like to you. I was hoping that nobody had seen us, that we could keep our relationship a secret until the time was right to share it with the world. Damn, this feels so awkward."

"It's okay, Claudia," said John, putting his hand on her knee. "I understand. I understand now, but I didn't understand then. I think I judged you too quickly. But I guess that's what happens when you only know one side of the story."

A snake slithers and weaves its spineless body through the desert. It flirts with the grains of sand as it casually tosses them aside, all the while etching its path into the dry, dusty landscape. On and on it goes, gliding sinuously from left to right and right to left. A gentle breeze breaks the blistering heat of the day, and like nature's broom, it exhales and sweeps away all evidence of the creature's journey and restores the wilderness to its perfect state of imperfection.

Claudia longed for her life to be that windswept landscape, for the path behind her to be smooth and untarnished by the memories that haunted her every waking moment.

She thought of Gareth, driving to the dam that evening, his emotions out of control, his world crumbling around him, his soul empty, his heart broken, a raging fire consuming him from the inside, and then, there in front of him, it appeared, its bright lights puncturing the darkness. He pushed his foot down hard on the accelerator. He closed his eyes, and he screamed.

CHAPTER 17

Indictment. The more Claudia tried to run from it, the more she felt its hot breath on her neck as it crept up closer towards her.

Acquaintances and strangers stood at the side of the lane that was her life, watching her every step, waiting for her to lose her footing and fall – to see her splayed out on the concrete like a hunted animal, shot down, convulsing and bleeding out.

But Claudia was not falling. She was flying.

She sat at a school concert that night alone, her first public event without Gareth, remembering how he would stand to the side with the video camera, waiting to capture the moment his boys stepped on stage.

She could feel the eyes boring into the back of her head. Glances quickly shifted away when she looked in their direction. The rumour mill was in overdrive. People wanted to see a little drama. Bored with their own lives, many took a callous pleasure in picking the pieces out of the lives of others. Claudia was a lesbian, and her inappropriate sexual desires had led her off the track and into the arms of another woman while she heartlessly extinguished the life of her husband to make room for her selfish happiness. Why else would there be no outward display of the mourning widow?

When she arrived at work the following morning, her colleague Frances told her about a dream she had had the night before, where Claudia had been at the airport with Gareth, waiting for a gift to arrive from her parents. She was so excited about this gift, and Gareth was standing next to her, smiling, a great big smile that spread across his face from ear to ear.

The gift, when it arrived, was a beautiful handwoven silk cushion.

Frances said that she had never dreamed about Claudia before but that it was such a happy, peaceful dream that she believed that Gareth was, perhaps, reaching out to Claudia through the dream in an attempt to let Claudia know that he was okay.

Ellie, another colleague, put her arms around Claudia and told her that the gift – the cushion – was a symbol of the new life that Claudia had been given.

Claudia fought back the tears. She thought about how much Gareth had loved her. She thought about the morning before he died when he rolled over in bed and told her that she was the best thing to ever have happened to him. She thought about how she had shrugged him off because she didn't want to hear it – because she knew that she could not echo his words.

Ellie drew Claudia in and hugged her tightly. "Claudia," she said, "you are a successful, independent and beautiful young woman. I'm certain that Gareth knew that if anything ever happened to him, or if you were to divorce, you would have been able to move on without him in a heartbeat. Gareth loved you too much. I think he felt completely bound to you, dependent on you even for his own happiness."

Ellie swallowed hard. "He probably knew in his soul that he would not have been able to continue his life without you in it. He couldn't see through the fog to imagine another way forward."

"I wish he had been able to," said Claudia. "He didn't even give it a chance."

Thinking about Frances' dream brought her a small measure of peace. Claudia knew that it was possible that the dead could communicate through the living. Perhaps he really was trying to reach out to her. But how on Earth, thought Claudia, could he be at peace, knowing what he knows now?

∞

Claudia sat bolt upright in bed. "Mommy!" Claudia heard the screams from downstairs. Blood-curdling screams. "Mommy, please come! *Mommeeeeeee!*"

She stumbled out of bed and, gripping the railing tightly in the dark, ran downstairs to Ross's room, where she found him sitting on the edge of his bed, wide-eyed and terrified. She switched on the bedside lamp and pulled him close to her.

"Mommy, I saw Daddy," he said breathlessly. "I saw Daddy!"

Claudia tried to calm herself.

"Ross, my darling, Daddy is in Heaven, you know that. Are you sure it was him?"

"I saw him, Mommy," said Ross, pointing outside. "He was right there outside my window."

Claudia stood up and walked to the window. She pulled the curtains open and looked outside. There was nobody there.

"I think you must have dreamed it, my boy," she said gently, sitting down next to him and putting her arms around his body. He was shaking.

"No, Mommy, it wasn't a dream. This was real. It was Daddy's head that I saw. His head was chopped off, and his face looked sore, and he was screaming outside my window. It was Daddy, I know my Daddy. Don't say it wasn't my Daddy!"

Claudia felt her body go cold. There was something special about Ross. He was incredibly intuitive and perceptive. Many of Claudia's more spiritual friends had referred to him as an Indigo Child. She could not discount what he was telling her, but she sure as hell didn't want to believe that it could be real.

Ross knew that his father had died in an accident, but he knew none of the details. He could not have read the accident report because she had carefully filed it away.

Was Gareth trying to reach out to his son, too?

Claudia hugged her little boy tightly.

"I don't want to sleep here alone, Mommy. I'm scared."

Kyle stood in the doorway, rubbing the sleep out of his eyes.

"Mom, are you guys okay?"

"We're okay, my darling," Claudia said, smiling. "Ross is just a little scared."

Kyle sat down on the bed and wrapped his arms protectively around his little brother.

"What scared you, Ross?" he asked.

"I saw Daddy's head outside my window. His head was chopped off. He was like an angry ghost, and he was screaming outside my window. I was so scared, Kyle."

Kyle looked at Claudia. Claudia bit her lower lip.

"Mom?"

"I think that maybe you should come upstairs and sleep in my bed tonight, Ross," said Claudia. "I will make you something warm to help you sleep."

Ross smiled and nodded, picking up his old, threadbare teddy bear and placing it under his arm. "Can Kyle come too, Mommy?"

"Of course, Kyle can come too," said Claudia, fighting back the tears.

"Mom, why would Dad come back to haunt us?" whispered Kyle once he was certain his brother was asleep. Claudia glanced down at Ross. He was sleeping peacefully.

"I don't know what Ross saw, my darling," she whispered back gently. "But I don't think that it was Dad. I'm sure that it was just a nightmare."

Claudia's communication with Alex over the past few couple of days had been watered down to a few text messages and the odd Facebook note. She felt guilty for having so little time available to see him. It was a treacherous road that she travelled as she tried to protect her children from her secret. Alex was acutely aware of this and was careful not to pressurise her into placing herself in an awkward position where she might feel the need to choose between him and her children.

September 12th, 11:21am

Alex Winterton

Darling, there is absolutely no rush to reach the finish line.

I know I have said this before, but the only thing more important than us is your two special children. They have lost their father, and the only one left for them is you. It is so important that you are present in their lives right now, loving them and being compassionate and aware of their feelings and needs. It is only through this that they will open up to you – and you to them.

Love them and be there for them.

Our time will come.

Speaking of which, I have discovered that I have the entire weekend all to myself. I am conscious of the boys and their time with you, but do you think that you could see your way clear for us to spend some of this precious time together, even if it is for an hour or two? I would love to sit down with you over a bottle of wine and ease the pain that you are feeling at the moment. Sometimes, just talking things through gives a situation a different perspective.

It was time to fetch the boys from school. Claudia knew that Denise would be there, and she wanted to spend a few moments with her before the school bell rang. She missed her friend terribly, and the rumours were not making matters any easier.

Denise waved when she saw Claudia walking towards her.

"Hey you!" she said warmly. "How are you feeling, my friend?"

"Split in two," said Claudia and sighed deeply. "The past couple of days have been incredibly trying. Poor little Ross has been taking so much strain. He woke up last night thinking he had seen Gareth's severed head outside his window."

"Oh my heavens, Claudia," said Denise, rubbing her arms as she felt a chill run through her body. "That's eerie."

"I know. I am still trying to figure out if that was a nightmare or if he really saw it."

"I'm sure it was a nightmare," said Denise. "His mind is probably drawing pictures of what Gareth must have looked like when he died."

"I guess."

The school bell rang, and children poured out of the classrooms.

"And then, to further complicate matters," said Claudia, raising her voice above the chatter, "everyone around here thinks that we're getting it on."

Denise laughed. "Let them believe what they want to believe, my friend. The only thing that matters is the truth, and we both know what that is."

"Mommy!" Claudia felt Ross as he collided with her and wrapped his arms around the back of her legs. She gave him a hug, and they all walked back to the car park together.

As the two friends said goodbye, Denise put her arms around Claudia and planted a big kiss on her friend's lips.

"I love you, my friend," she said, and then, lowering her voice, she whispered into Claudia's ear. "And I hope everyone saw that!"

∞

There was an email from the local scout group waiting for her when she returned to the office.

It was an invitation for Kyle and Ross to attend a campout in the Magaliesburg that weekend.

"Would you boys like to go camping this weekend?" Claudia asked as she popped her head into the lounge. The boys were jostling for a spot on the giant, green beanbag in front of the television, and Kyle's arm froze in mid-air, about to deliver a punch to his little brother's ribs in an attempt to claim his space.

Claudia cleared her throat, and Kyle lowered his arm and grinned sheepishly.

"It's a scouting camp," she explained. "Songs by the fire, stalk the lantern, all the things you love."

"Please, please, please, can we go, Mommy!" squealed Ross. "And I want to take a *big* bag of marshmallows to toast."

"And you, Kyle?" Claudia asked, concerned about the darkness that clouded his face.

Kyle shrugged his shoulders. "Will you be okay on your own, Mom? I'm scared to leave you all alone."

"I'll be just fine," she said, smiling, grateful for his concern. "Besides, it would be good for the two of you to get out into the bush a bit and take your mind off things, don't you think?"

"Are you sure, Mom?" asked Kyle again.

"Pinky promise," said Claudia, lifting the little finger on her right hand up and extending it towards her son.

Kyle hooked his little finger in hers and grinned. "Okay, Mom, but if you get lonely, you must promise that you will fetch us. Deal?"

"Deal."

September 13th, 8:26 am

Claudia Stevenson

Alex, thank you for your beautiful words. Thank you for being so unselfish and for allowing me and the boys the space we need to come to terms with what has happened. This time together is going to stand us in good stead in the years to come.

One of my colleagues at the office gave me a candle this morning together with a card that read When things get dark and a little rough, hold on to the light. The first thing I thought of was you, the true light in my life.

The boys received a letter today inviting them to a scouting camp this weekend, and they both really want to go. Once again, it seems that the Universe has found a way for us to be together.

I can hardly wait.

I love you so damn much.

Claudia had spoken to Lynne, a client who was also a child psychologist, later that afternoon. She had enquired about the boys and how they were coping with the trauma of their father's death.

Listening to Claudia talking about Ross' nightmare, she suggested that Claudia send Kyle and Ross to a few play therapy sessions.

"You don't want them acting out or becoming dysfunctional teenagers if they haven't been able to process what they've been through," she said warmly.

Claudia, who had been so busy trying to put the disturbing event as far to the back of her mind as she could – using Alex as her primary distraction – felt embarrassed that she had not considered smoothing the path ahead for her children through any form of professional therapy. Other than Ross' nightmare, the children seemed to be moving on quite normally.

"Children don't always know how to express how they are feeling," explained Lynne. "Sometimes they just don't know how to verbalise what is going on in their heads, and so what often happens is they become aggressive or withdrawn because they have not been able to process the trauma they experienced in a way that makes sense to them."

"And play therapy would help them do this?" Claudia asked.

"Most definitely, Claudia. I've worked with hundreds of traumatised children over the years. Honestly, this is the best thing you can do for your children right now. Nip it in the bud before it becomes a psychological problem in the future."

Claudia thought back to her own childhood. Although she had not experienced anything close to what her children had been forced to experience, her childhood had been a tangled mess of confusion and uncertainty, cloaked in a veil of emotional, verbal, and sometimes physical abuse. Watching her mother descending into a state of genetically induced schizophrenia, she remembered grabbing her brother's hand on many occasions and just running, slamming the gate and running down the road as fast as they could to escape the madness.

Sometimes, they would run the twelve to thirteen miles to their father's home, and he would pack them into his car and take them back home a little later, and then there were times when they would stop running. They would turn around and walk back home. Either way, the madness never left them.

On one occasion, Claudia's mother had sent her down to the shops to buy frozen fish for the cats. Claudia had come back with the wrong brand and, in a fit of fury, her mother had hurled the frozen box at Claudia. Claudia felt her ears ringing as she fell to the ground, the impact toppling her over, her head smashing down hard against the paving.

She wobbled to her feet, and she ran. She ran until she couldn't see her mother or the house or the stupid box of fish. She turned a corner in the road, sat down on the curb and sobbed.

Once the crying had subsided, she stood up and ran again. She ran past the cemetery, cars and buses and hooting taxis whizzing past her on the road. She ran past the shopping centre. The church. The public swimming baths. She was thirsty, but she kept on running. A few hours later, she arrived at her father's home, exhausted and dehydrated. She scratched at the dried blood that had formed on her forehead, not realising that her head had been cut open.

As she lay in the back seat of her father's car on the way back from the doctor's rooms – being diagnosed as having suffered a mild concussion from the blow – she overheard her stepmother saying softly to her father, "We have to get those children out of there."

Claudia cringed as she relived that moment. She had spent the greater part of her adult life trying to process her childhood, learning to forgive and move on. It had not been easy. In fact, she occasionally found herself trapped in a downward spiral of guilt and anger and hurt when she thought back to her life with her mother. How she wished she could go back and start again.

Claudia thought about her two precious children. She had wrapped them in her wings since they were tiny babies, promising herself that they would never be exposed to a life of insanity or suffering on any level. That they would never, ever feel as if it was them against the world. And yet here they were, bobbing about in an ocean of craziness that Claudia could never have envisioned for them. She ached to grab the pen that was writing her life and scratch out all the hurt and the pain and the confusion.

She called Lynne and booked a series of play therapy sessions for the boys for the following week.

"You're doing the right thing, Claudia," Lynne said on the other end of the line. "You are sparing them years of psychological and emotional issues."

"Thank you, Lynne. I really appreciate this," Claudia said warmly.

"You're a good mother, you know that?" Lynne reminded her.

Claudia felt her soul recoiling.

A good mother doesn't take their children's father away from them, she thought.

CHAPTER 18

With their noses pressed up against the windows of the bus and their faces disappearing behind the steam forming from their warm breath on the glass, Claudia waved goodbye to Ross and Kyle as they set off on their camp.

She sat down in her car, enjoying the early morning sun that filtered in through her windscreen and warmed the side of her face. She breathed in deeply, fighting back the tears that engulfed her.

"Please, God," she prayed out loud, "please let them be okay. Please protect their bus and get them to the camp safely."

The aftermath of a traumatic event is a double-edged sword.

On the one side, it is quiet and unassuming, like the mist that rises off a lake on a cold winter's morning. Vapour droplets dance in a slow, melancholic rhythm, colliding and clinging on to each other in a desperate attempt to remain suspended in time, but the sun's rays draw them upwards, luring them towards her bright, warm light, until eventually they have disappeared into nothingness.

That's the one side of trauma. People get over it. They move on. The resilience of the human spirit propels them forward, sending them hurtling into new places and spaces where they find themselves again.

But on the other side of this sword is something darker. Like a thick fog, this side swallows and suffocates everything it touches. As it sinks, it creeps into the crevices of the soul and fills each open crack with anxiety and dread. The victim stands alone, shrouded in its asphyxiating grasp, a casualty of circumstance, uncertain of whether they are trapped within the fog or whether it is trapped within them.

Claudia felt the suffocating dread consuming her. She started the engine, lurched the car into first gear and pushed her foot down hard on the accelerator, racing towards the bus. If she could just stay close enough, she thought, she would know that they were safe from harm. It was a warped sense of assurance that she would not be punished by the cruel hand of fate too soon, punished for her infidelity, the possibility of discovery playing over and over again like a sickening loop in a horror film.

The bus turned off the main road and onto the dirt road that led to the campsite. Claudia slowed down on the side of the road and watched the dry dust that had been kicked up by the bus tumble and twirl its way through the air, settling in a thin film on her car. She switched the engine off and waited for the air to clear. She breathed in deeply and gritted her teeth.

"Hold it together, Claudia," she said to herself. "For God's sake, hold it together."

Claudia returned to the house to pack a few more boxes into her car to take out to the holiday house before she left to meet with Alex later.

The house was quiet without the children. A disturbing coolness had settled on everything. Claudia looked around at the photographs on the walls, years of shared memories with Gareth frozen in time.

She removed them one by one, covering them in newspaper and placing them in an unmarked box. She taped the box closed and wrote his name on the top in large capital letters:

GARETH

She knew that she would never open that box again.

∞

She tried to avoid driving that way, past the place where it all happened. When she did, she would feel a pickling coldness overcome her. The closer she got to the place where he had died, the stronger the sensation became. She would feel the shortness of her breath as her pulse quickened, and she would press her foot down hard on the accelerator so that she could emerge from that strange twilight zone as quickly as possible.

Claudia wondered if Gareth was still standing there beside the mess, wondering what the hell had happened, rooted to the ground in disbelief.

The crumpled metal remains of his car had been removed, the shards of glass had been swept up, and the oil was just another stain on the side of the road. The evidence was gone, but he was still there. Forgotten. People drove past the landmark where his life was abruptly halted, oblivious. Funny that. How everybody just goes back to their business. It hadn't been quite what he had expected.

There had been an accident on the highway that she generally took when she wanted to avoid driving the road that took her past the scene of Gareth's death.

"Damn it," she thought as she saw the sea of brake lights ahead of her. She quickly made a U-turn and drove back towards the hairpin bend that would take her back home the other way.

As she drove closer to where Gareth had taken his last breath, she felt the coldness creeping into her car and under her skin. Claudia looked up into the darkening sky and begged out loud, "Please, Gareth, please leave this terrible place. You don't belong here anymore. There's nothing left here for you."

She felt dizzy. Why would he listen to her anyway? She didn't even know if it was Gareth that she was feeling. Perhaps it was just her own stupid guilt. But it was so bloody cold. Her guilt was hot and fiery, and it cut through her like a knife. The coldness was different. It clung to her like a heavy fog.

Alex. Kyle. Ross. Claudia held on to them like a patient in a mental asylum clings on to their sanity. Claudia was terrified of losing her grip on reality.

The boys were safe, that she knew, and Alex was on his way. Once again, she closed her eyes and prayed, this time for Alex's safety, that she would not be punished a second time by having something happen to him while he was on his way to her.

She wished that she could muffle her crazy thoughts, but they knocked on the doors inside her head persistently and always found a way to get in.

They had the master key, and they could open as many doors as they pleased.

Claudia closed the curtains and dimmed the lights. She struck a match and watched the flame as it burst into life, crackling as it hungrily consumed itself. She lit two candles and watched the flames sway in unison, their shadows playing with each other on the wall.

A freshly uncorked bottle of wine was waiting breathlessly on the counter. Claudia arranged the cheese on a white platter, Camembert and Brie, melting from the outside in, like ice cream served from a warm scoop. She placed a bowl of preserved figs and sweet, pungent crystallised ginger on the table and drizzled extra virgin olive oil and balsamic vinegar into a small bowl. She broke warm, crusty chunks of bread onto another board and crowned the presentation with a sculpted snowdrift of golden butter.

Andrea Bocelli played softly in the background, his voice pregnant with emotion. Claudia watched the curtains rising and falling in the cool spring breeze while she waited for the lights of Alex's car to appear outside. Her body, her heart and her soul were aching for him. Claudia wondered, with a strange sense of guilty pleasure, what stories would unfold on this beautiful night.

Alex's head appeared around the side of the curtain, and Claudia felt the blood rush to her cheeks as Alex grinned naughtily at her.

"Hello, my darling," whispered Claudia, her cheeks flushed and her pulse racing.

Claudia and Alex embraced, their bodies pressed against each other, their lips touching, parting, tongues searching.

Alex ran his hands through her hair and traced his index finger around the side of her face.

"Hello, beautiful," he said. "I've missed you so much."

"I'm so glad you're finally here," smiled Claudia, hugging him close to her.

Forcing themselves apart, Claudia pointed to the feast that she had prepared.

"Let's tuck in. Tonight, I'm going to feed your soul."

The hours melted away. Claudia lay with Alex on the couch, resting between his legs, her back against his chest, his soft breath tickling her neck, and they spoke about the week that had been and the emotional mountains that they were both climbing.

Alex switched the mood of the music to the vulnerable, sacred and mysterious voice of Sinéad O'Connor and, taking Claudia's hand, he pulled her up towards him. With his arms wrapped around her waist and hers around his neck, they danced. Slowly. Sensually. Deliberately.

It was not long before they were entangled in a blood-rushing, heart-racing embrace that neither could – nor wanted to – stop.

"Alex," whispered Claudia, "I could make love to you right now."

She felt Alex's body press closer to hers, "I want you so much, Claudia," he said, his breathing heavy and his pulse racing, surrendering to her suggestion.

Alex took Claudia by the hand and led her to the bedroom. Claudia unbuttoned his shirt and peeled it from his body, and Alex ran his hands up her waist, raising her arms above her head as he removed her sweater. Guiding her towards the bed, Alex deftly slipped the remainder of her clothes from her body. Claudia ran her hands along his belt and unclipped the buckle. She could feel him throbbing, almost uncontrollably, beneath her hands.

Together, they lay down, their bodies aching for each other. They both looked at each other, wide-eyed, the thrill of what they were about to do, years of yearning melting away before them, palpable and intense. The passion surged between them. Alex slowly brought his body down towards Claudia. Their eyes met, and they both smiled at each other and then suddenly, he was inside her, thrusting himself deeper and deeper, their bodies both aching with the intensity of the pleasure.

"We're finally making love," whispered Alex as his eyes locked with Claudia, and Claudia pulled Alex towards her, her nails digging into his buttocks.

"Oh God, Alex, and what beautiful love this is!"

Their bodies moved in unison, their eyes both wide with anticipation, still smiling at each other. It was the moment they had both been waiting for. Claudia gasped as she felt her body shudder as she began to climax.

"Alex!" she cried, and Alex pushed down harder, thrusting himself deep inside her, intensifying her pleasure. The sensation was too much to bear, and before Alex could hold back any longer, he was climaxing, too. He threw his head back in ecstasy and let out a deep moan as his body shook and convulsed, and the waves of pleasure pulsated through him.

As the night progressed, the lovemaking became even more passionate.

"Turn over onto your back, Alex," said Claudia, smiling, her skin glowing.

She straddled him, her legs pressing tightly against his hip bones while she ran her hands over the curves of his body. Alex groaned as he felt himself slowly sliding inside her. Claudia lowered herself towards him and teasingly ran her tongue across his lips until, once more, he felt his body beginning to shake. He closed his eyes and arched his back, and his breathing grew faster, and Claudia pushed down hard against him. Together, in that precious moment in time, Alex and Claudia were the entire Universe, and around them, galaxies collided and exploded into millions of little pieces.

Claudia lay next to Alex, watching him sleep peacefully beside her. It had been beyond all imagination. Everything had connected so perfectly.

As the sun rose on the horizon the following morning, Claudia was woken from her sleep with Alex's chest against her back, his breathing heavy as he kissed the back of her neck, his body trembling with desire. She pushed herself close to him and felt his hardness throbbing against her, and she gently guided him inside her.

Two worlds had collided, and as surreal as it felt in that moment, there was no turning back.

The missing piece of the puzzle had been slotted into place.

CHAPTER 19

Uneasiness. It creeps in under the skin and closes its icy fingers around the heart's tender arteries and pinches until the pulsating rhythm slows down, and then slowly, very slowly, the blood runs cold.

The mind has an uncanny way of prompting us to sit up and take notice when something is not quite right.

Gareth's parents were bitter and angry. They were trapped in their heart-wrenching denial and clung to the sadness like a tick clings to its host, drawing on its life force until, swollen and bloated, it capitulates and falls to the ground in a state of self-digesting gluttony.

But his parents could not let go. Falling would mean accepting. It was easier to be trapped in a downward spiral than it would be to release the liability they had attached to their former daughter – in-law and move on without the abhorrence that consumed them. Oh, how they hated Claudia. It should have been her that died that night.

They persisted unrelentingly in their pursuit to hold on to their precious grandchildren, the only remaining ties to their son.

They wanted the children. Claudia could not help but wonder how far they were prepared to go.

Claudia's father had warned her not to let the boys anywhere near their grandparents, at least not until they had calmed down – when they had stopped playing the blame game.

Claudia felt ill. Gareth's father had just called. He had changed his number, and Claudia had unsuspectingly taken the call. Avoiding their calls was easier than having to deal with a confrontation. An awkward request. A cynical suggestion.

He asked to take the children for one night.

Just one night.

Children are like sponges. A few hours in the company of their grandparents could herald the beginning of a cycle of torturous brainwashing.

Claudia felt as if a sock had been shoved into her mouth.

She agreed.

Shit, why had she agreed, she thought as she watched the words walking out of her mouth.

Shit.

Claudia could not afford to have her children conditioned in any way. The guilt was already too much to bear without having it fed intravenously into their brains by the very people who were determined to perpetuate it. But she had agreed. She had stepped into the abyss, and there was no turning back.

You fool, she thought. You bloody fool.

∞

Claudia's mobile phone was ringing.

"Mom,' shouted Kyle, running through the house holding her phone, "Your phone is ringing!"

"Who is it?" Claudia asked.

"It says ARW," said Kyle, handing her the phone.

Alex Rhys Winterton.

"Thank you, my boy," she said. "I'll see you in a few minutes."

"Hello, my darling," she said, closing the bedroom door and leaning up against it. "It's so good to hear your voice again."

∞

Claudia laughed as she watched Ross fighting a strand of molten cheese from his toasted sandwich as it held on for dear life, stretching like an elastic band and dribbling all over his chin.

"You're going to get yourself tangled up in that if you don't chomp it off," said Claudia as Ross wrapped the gooey cheese around his index finger and shoved it into his mouth.

"There. All gone," giggled Ross through mouthfuls of crumbs, licking his fingers voraciously.

"So, Mom," asked Kyle inquisitively, "who was that person you were speaking to earlier?"

"On the phone?" asked Claudia, swallowing hard, trying to prolong answering his question.

"Yes, that AWR person," he reminded her.

"You mean ARW?" asked Claudia, instantly wishing that she had not gone there.

"Well, whoever, ARW then," said Kyle, smiling.

"Just a friend, my darling. But it's no one that you know."

"Is he single?" Kyle asked.

Claudia felt the blood rushing to her feet.

"How do you know that this person is a man?" she asked tentatively.

"I just know," said Kyle.

"Okay, so you're right, it is a man, but he's just a friend."

Kyle smiled. Knowingly.

"So, who's up for another toasted cheese then?" she asked, leaping out of her chair and pouncing on Kyle, smothering him with kisses and laughing as he doubled over in hysterics.

Claudia could not bring herself to tell Kyle and Ross about the upcoming visit to their grandparents. As the distance grew between the families, so did the terror in her children. Ross was particularly nervous, the image of his grandmother, irrationally twisted and wild, attacking Claudia and being dragged out of the house still fresh in his mind.

Claudia kicked herself for agreeing to the visit. She knew that she was potentially placing her children in danger. Questions would be fired at them in an attempt to dig for clues, to expose cracks in Claudia's carefully constructed system, trapping them in a suffocating web of lies and turning them against her and everything she had worked so darn hard to keep together.

She gritted her teeth and sighed. "Shit."

Claudia and Alex chatted on Skype later that evening. These were stolen moments with precious little time but cherished nonetheless.

Alex: *So tell me, did the boys figure out who was on the phone?*

Claudia: *Well, it's funny that you should ask.*

Alex: *Tell me?*

Claudia: *Kyle asked me who was on the phone. So I told him that it was just a friend.*

Claudia: *And then he asked me if you were single. So I asked him how he knew that this friend was a guy. And he just said that he knew it was a guy.*

Alex: *Kids hey?*

Claudia: *But he wasn't upset or anything. It was just a cute conversation.*

Alex: *And he didn't pursue it from there?*

Claudia: *I changed the subject. I didn't want him thinking too much about things that he is not yet ready to deal with. But knowing what he knows will make it easier for me to break the ice one day when I tell him about us.*

Alex: *And it will make things easier for Ross, too.*

Claudia: *Exactly. But for now, it will remain the world's best-kept secret.*

Alex: *For as long as it needs to be that way.*

Alex: *P.S. I really miss you.*

Claudia: *I miss you so much, too. Sometimes, I just feel like telling you to drop what you're doing and meet me somewhere. Anywhere. Like right now.*

Alex: *I was thinking exactly the same thing today. I thought about rocking up at the dam and calling you and saying, "Meet me in the forest for a quick kiss and a hug". That would throw you, wouldn't it?*

∞

"It's just one night," Claudia pleaded.

Ross was shaking his head furiously. "No, Mommy, you can't make me go there."

"They love you, my boy," she implored. "You and Kyle are all they have left of your dad."

"I'm scared, Mommy. I'm scared of Grandma."

"I know. You saw some terrible things, and now you cannot forget them. Grandma would never hurt you. She is just angry with me."

The play therapy sessions were going well, and Lynne, to Claudia's relief, had assured Claudia that the memories of the night of Gareth's death, although painful and traumatic, were not going to cause Ross and Kyle any permanent psychological damage. It would just take time. Losing their father would always remain a gaping hole in their lives. It is a space so sacred that it is impossible for it to be filled by anyone or anything else. There are no substitutes for the parent wrenched from a child's life. Claudia knew that she would need to find the strength within her to be both mother and father to her sons. Gareth had left a set of incredibly difficult shoes to fill.

"If anything happens, Kyle will phone me, and I will be right there. I promise you that, my darling." Claudia said, taking Ross' little hand in her own. "I would never allow anything bad to happen to you."

"Can you fetch us early in the morning?" Ross pleaded.

"I will be there as soon as you've finished your breakfast. Besides, you can't be late for school," Claudia said and squeezed the back of Ross' neck.

Ross shivered and grinned, "Okay, mommy. But promise to be early."

"I promise."

"Pinky promise," Kyle piped up as he zipped his suitcase closed.

"Double pinky promise," Claudia laughed, reaching out and entwining her fingers around Kyle's.

The mood was cool as she arrived at her former in-law's home. Claudia fought the urge to reverse out of the driveway and take leave with the children.

There was a chilled but polite exchange of pleasantries as Claudia hugged her children goodbye.

"God, I hope I'm doing the right thing," she whispered under her breath.

"I will see you early tomorrow morning," she said, drawing a cross on Ross' chest as she kneeled down in front of her little boy.

"I love you, Mom," said Kyle, wrapping his arms around her neck.

"I love you too, sweetheart," she said, smiling, trying to avoid the glares of Gareth's parents. "And you too, you little monkey," she said, squeezing Ross' hand.

"God, please keep them safe," Claudia prayed as she drove away. "Please keep them safe."

She felt scared. Lonely. Powerless. She could not shake the feeling that she had made a terrible mistake. She had to find it within her to believe that Gareth's parents would not bring any harm to her children, that any feelings of malice would not be directed at them but at her.

Arriving at home, Claudia walked up to her front door and noticed a light burning in the kitchen. Had she forgotten to switch it off when she left that morning? Possibly. She turned her key in the lock. But the door was already unlocked. She felt her heart lurch in her chest. Had she forgotten to lock the house as well? Was she going crazy?

She pulled the sliding door open and scanned the room.

There on the kitchen counter was a bottle of wine, two glasses, and a long-stemmed red rose.

"Alex?" she whispered, "Are you here?"

Silence.

Nothing.

"Is *anybody* here?" she said, raising her voice slightly and backing towards the door.

"I'm right here," Alex whispered as he snuck up behind her, kissing the back of her neck and putting his arms around her. "I couldn't bear to have you spend the night alone."

∞

Claudia's mind was racked with thoughts of her children, and she drifted in and out of sleep as one dark hour stretched into another.

She must have fallen asleep because she suddenly woke up, her heart racing. She sat bolt upright in bed, trembling.

"Are you okay, my angel?" murmured Alex, placing his arms around her.

"I had the most awful dream, Alex," Claudia said, her voice shaking. "I went to fetch the boys from their grandparents, but when I arrived, the house was empty. Ross and Kyle were gone. I was running around the perimeter of the house in a state of panic. They had been taken, and it was too late for me to do anything."

Claudia felt the tears welling in her eyes.

"Alex, I hope they are okay. I hope they don't think I abandoned them."

"Would you like to drive through there now?" he asked gently.

Claudia dried her eyes, "Right now? What time is it?"

"It's 2 am."

"Maybe I should. Even if I just stand outside the house and make sure that nothing is out of place. I know that if they were going to disappear with the boys, they would take everything with them."

"I'm coming with you," said Alex.

"No, Alex," Claudia protested. "You know you can't do that."

"What if I follow you in my car? That way, I would still be close by if anything happened. And if you need to leave with the boys, then I could just drive home. But at least I would know that you are safe."

"Are you sure?" Claudia asked. "It's a long drive from here."

"Of course, I'm sure," said Alex. "Come on, let's get some clothes on. I'll make you a cup of coffee for the road."

Alex stopped at a nearby intersection while Claudia drove towards Gareth's parent's home. She pulled up alongside the kerb a couple of metres away from their front gate. God forbid they were awake and saw her spying on them, she thought.

The outside light was burning brightly, and the curtains were drawn closed.

Claudia squinted in the dark, her eyes searching the property for clues.

Everything was so darn quiet.

An early morning breeze began to blow, and Claudia felt a chill run through her body. It was so dark.

"Damn it," she thought. "I can't see a thing."

A car drove past the house, and the driver looked directly at her, slowed down, and then reversed back up the road towards her.

"Is everything okay, ma'am?" he asked, winding down his window.

Claudia grimaced.

"Yes, everything is fine, thank you. I've just locked myself out of the house."

She waved her mobile phone in the air above her head so that he could see it.

"Somebody is on their way to open up for me."

"Okeydokey," he said. "Do you want me to wait with you until they arrive?"

"I'll be fine," said Claudia, wishing that he would hurry up and leave. "Really, please don't worry about me."

"Be safe out there, ma'am," he said. "You never know who's prowling the streets at this hour."

Claudia waved him away, and as she did, she heard a thudding noise coming towards her. Within a matter of seconds, it was in front of her, growling and barking.

"Oh, Sassy," Claudia whispered, realising who it was. "*Shhhhh*, it's just me."

She reached her hand in through the gate and patted the dog as he whimpered and licked her hand, realising that she was not a threat.

Claudia looked up and noticed that the sky was brighter. The clouds that had covered the moon had blown away, and suddenly, there it was, the sign that she had been hoping for. A glint of metal reflected off the moonlight. It was Gareth's parents' car, parked up against the garage. They were at home.

She sighed and steadied herself on her feet. Her boys were safe.

With her heart thumping in her chest, Claudia drove her car back to the intersection where she had left Alex. He wound down his window as she approached. Claudia waved at him and smiled.

"The boys are okay, and everyone is there, including the family dog."

Alex smiled broadly.

"Thank goodness," he said. "What a relief."

"Let's go home," said Claudia.

Alex revved his engine and grinned at her. "Race you back!"

∞

When Claudia arrived at Gareth's parent's home the following morning, Kyle and Ross were waiting at the front door.

Safe and sound.

Unharmed.

Claudia felt ridiculous.

"Did you have a good time?" she asked as she looked back at them in the rear view mirror.

"It was okay, Mom," said Kyle, "Grandma and Grandpa are so sad. They just cried the whole time."

"Ah, my boy," said Claudia, sensing their pain. "Did they speak about Dad at all?"

"That's all they spoke about," said Kyle. "They showed us all these old photos of him. Look," he said, pulling an envelope out of his blazer pocket, "they even gave us some of the photos."

"That's nice of them," said Claudia, knowing that it was going to be these small treasures that kept the memory of their father alive.

"I miss Dad," said Ross quietly.

"Me too," said Kyle as he ran his hand across one of the photos, outlining his father's face.

"I miss Dad too, my boys," said Claudia. "I wish things didn't have to be like this."

∞

A speck on the landscape. That's all they really were. Three souls tumbling and turning inside their human bodies, trying to make sense of the world. Claudia was at the wheel, lost in thought.

Kyle and Ross sat in the back, staring outside as they watched life race past their windows in a dizzying blur.

The silence was punctuated by the ringing of her mobile phone. She fumbled around in her handbag on the passenger seat and pulled it out. It was Alex. She glanced back at the boys, debating whether or not she should take the call.

"Are you going to answer that, Mom?" asked Kyle.

Claudia nodded and answered the phone. "I've got it."

September 24th, 20:50 pm

Claudia Stevenson

My darling Alex, I must be honest, I didn't think that I would be writing to you tonight, but I had the most profound experience this evening that I couldn't possibly express over the telephone. I am not sure how you are going to respond to what I am about to tell you, but I am going to share this with you nonetheless.

After we ended our telephone conversation earlier, Kyle asked me who I was talking to, and Ross piped up, "It's Grace, silly!" And Kyle said no, it wasn't Grace, and he asked me again. So I told him that it was a friend, a very special friend.

We carried on driving for a while when we both noticed that Ross had fallen asleep. Kyle then asked me about you again, and what he said threw me completely. He looked at me, smiled, and said, "Mom, am I ever going to meet this special friend of yours?"

I couldn't believe what he had just said. And I said, "Of course, my angel – when the time is right."

And he said to me, "This person really makes you happy, doesn't he?"

And I just smiled and said, "Yes, he does, very much so."

He asked where I knew you from, so I told him all about our past, and he laughed and said how cool that was. And then I told him that we had reconnected recently, a few weeks before his dad had died, and that at that stage, we were just friends. I told him how much you had helped me deal with everything after Gareth died, and once again, he smiled and told me how cool that was.

Then he looked at me – and as he did, I took my foot off the accelerator so that I could slow down the passage of time and just take the entirety of that moment in – and said to me, "Mom, I couldn't wish for a better mom, and if I had to choose another mom, I wouldn't ever be able to, because you are the best mom in the whole world."

I caught myself holding my breath, and then he said to me, "I can see how happy you are when you talk to this person, and I really want you to be happy. And I'm not going to be cross if you find someone to replace Dad because I just want you to be happy."

My heart was breaking for this little boy, wise beyond his years, opening his heart up to me like this.

In between my attempts to hold back my tears, I said to him, "My boy, I would never want to jeopardise the special relationship we share, and no one will ever come between us."

He laughed and said, "This guy sounds really cool."

And I said, "Yes, he is, and he makes me laugh."

And then Kyle asked, "So, Mom, is he a negative person?"

And I smiled and said, "He's everything but negative. In fact, he is probably one of the most positive people I know!"

And he said, "Cool."

And then he said again, "I just want you to be happy, Mom. And if he makes you happy, then I am happy."

I cannot begin to express how my soul soared at that moment. He was giving me his blessing, Alex. He was giving us his blessing.

And then he asked me, "Is this the person you've been hiding from me with all your text messages? And every time you click out of the screen on your computer when I walk past you?"

And I said, "Yes, my boy, but I was doing that to protect you because I don't want you to get the wrong idea and think that I'd forgotten about your Dad."

And he said to me, "Don't worry, Mom, I know you would never hurt us."

"Promise me that this is your secret and my secret," I asked. "Nobody needs to know about this right now, especially your grandparents."

And he crossed his heart and hoped to die, "Stick a needle in my eye," he said and promised me that he wouldn't tell a soul.

And once again told me how happy he was for me.

I told him that he will meet you someday soon, but that right now, I want to focus on spending as much quality time with him and Ross as possible until I know that they are both strong enough and ready to welcome somebody new into their lives.

He just seemed so happy and content. And I felt so happy and content.

I am still trying to get my head around the fact that the one little person who is so sensitive, who I thought would really struggle with the thought of me moving on with somebody else, had given me not only one but two thumbs up, and who was genuinely excited about the future.

What a beautiful end to a day.

The things that hit us out of left field…

While I was sitting typing this to you, Kyle was in the bath, and he asked me what your name was.

So I told him that I wasn't going to tell him just yet and that once again when the time is right, he will know and see all.

And he was content with that.

I love this road that we're on, my baby, with all its bumps. I know that the destination is going to be so worth the ride...

September 24th, 23:41 pm

Alex Winterton

My angel,

How fantastic is that? I am sitting here typing to you, and at the same time, I am wiping the tears from my eyes and sniffing a little. And there I was, asking you if he had any clue. Sherlock Holmes pieces the whole thing together with such love, care and total consideration for the special woman in his life. I am so glad you handled everything the way you did, and you are right, the timing of the Universe will allow all things to unfold to everyone, just as it perfectly intends.

Thank you so much for sharing this special moment with me and for allowing me to be such a huge part of your life.

I love you so very much.

CHAPTER 20

Darkness. A strip of cloth tied around the head, blotting out the light. Patterns and shapes weave their way through the thin lines of intermeshed thread, but until the blindfold is removed, the world on the other side remains fuzzy and indistinct.

Standing outside a house, listening to the noises emanating from the four walls that enclose those who live behind them, sifting through clues, signs and symbols, we think that it is possible to construct a picture of what is going on behind those closed doors. We paint our own pictures. We sign our names at the bottom. We frame them. But those pictures are merely an artist's impression of what we believe to be real.

Claudia dialled her sister-in-law Sophia's number. They had not spoken since the day Andrew had arrived to collect Gareth's belongings from the house. Sophia had not judged Claudia in the same way that the rest of the family had judged her, but there was so much that had been left unsaid.

It was their son's sixteenth birthday. Claudia had been part of his life for most of those sixteen years. Even though she had been excommunicated from the family, Claudia felt compelled to call her nephew and wish him a happy birthday. Besides, she needed to reconnect with Sophia somehow.

"Hello, Claudia," Sophia said warmly as she answered the phone. "This is a nice surprise."

There were a few minutes of awkward small talk, a pause while Claudia wished her nephew a happy birthday, a stilted silence, a thought to perhaps end the conversation, and then, like a feather falling to the floor and suddenly catching a breath of wind and being lifted up, the conversation took flight again.

"How are things going?" asked Sophia. "How are they *really* going?"

Claudia swallowed hard.

"They're going okay, I guess, but it's still early days."

"Claudia, I have only heard one side of the story about Gareth. There are too many things that don't add up. Please tell me *your* side of the story?"

Claudia knew that mentioning Alex at this point would be too risky and kept the focus of the conversation on Gareth. She removed Sophia's blindfold and let in the light. She opened the door and showed Sophia the world she had shared with her husband.

Sophia listened with an open mind. She did not judge. A sense of relief flooded into the conversation.

"I didn't know Claudia," she said, sighing. "I really had no idea. I am so sorry."

"You weren't supposed to know anything, Sophia," Claudia said kindly. "We kept the tumultuous side of our marriage under lock and key. I guess we both thought that perhaps one day we would work things out. We didn't want to admit that our marriage was over, not even to each other."

"I know," Sophia sympathised, "it's not as if Andrew and I haven't been through some really tough times in all the years that we have been married."

"I'm so glad that you and Andrew worked things out," said Claudia. "In fact, do you remember when you came to visit us in December, and you and I were standing in the kitchen, and you were telling me how happy you were and how in love you were with him?"

"Of course I remember that. I remember how you burst out crying when I said those words."

"I told you how lucky you were to be so happy, Sophia," said Claudia. "And I said that I wished

I was you because Gareth and I were not in love, and we certainly were not happy."

"I remember that."

"Sophia, that was the first time that I had actually admitted to anyone in the family that I was deeply unhappy. But I still clung on to the hope that I could save my marriage, that I could get the old Gareth back. He was just so damn bitter about everything. I knew that there was no way that I could fix him and make him happy again. He'd pushed me way beyond the point of loving him again."

"I know the family is hell-bent on blaming you for Gareth's unhappiness," said Sophia. "But I don't believe it for one second. In my heart, I believe that he felt like a complete failure on the day he died. Between his business and his deteriorating marriage, what you said to him that morning must have pushed him over the edge. I don't think he was thinking rationally when he got into his car that day. I think he was being reckless and lost control of his car."

Claudia told her about the brake marks that had been left behind on the road.

"I don't think that somebody who was trying to end their life would have slammed on the brakes," said Sophia. "Unless he changed his mind in those split seconds before he collided with that truck. By then, it would have been too late."

Claudia found her mind wandering back to the day she collected the accident report from the police station. There were so many unanswered questions. Was it suicide? Or was it a freak accident? Did he live up to the threat that he had shared with John? Did he feel so hopeless that he saw no escape route other than death? Was his life over before the final impact, but he wanted to make sure that Claudia would carry the burden of her decision for the rest of her life?

"I know that I will go to the grave with this, Sophia," said Claudia sadly. "I wish I knew the truth. I really want to believe that it was an accident."

John's words flooded her veins.

She could not bring herself to share John's secret with her sister-in-law. There were already too many nails in her coffin, and she did not want to destroy the remaining tiny beacon of hope that the family clung on to, that Gareth's death was not a suicide, that Gareth was just in the wrong place at the wrong time; a more comforting thought than believing that he had lost all hope in carrying on.

Claudia expressed her concerns about Gareth's parents and her fear that they might attempt to brainwash Kyle and Ross and turn them against her or, worse still, take them away from her.

"Claudia, please do not worry about that," said Sophia with absolute sincerity. "All they want is to have access to the small piece of Gareth that lives on in his children. Believe me, they know that if they jeopardised the relationship by saying something inappropriate, you could cut ties with them immediately, and by doing that, they would lose their last glimmer of hope. I really don't think that they would risk taking that chance."

"I really want to believe you," said Claudia. "I'm terrified that the more time the boys spend with their grandparents, the more likely it is that the walls will crumble. Once something has been said, it is very difficult to reverse the damage of those words. Children are so trusting, and I don't want Kyle and Ross being fed the wrong information."

"Just give it time," said Sophia. "You'll see, they mean no harm."

∞

Pain is a funny thing. It can swallow you whole and spit you out in pieces, leaving you to hurriedly retrieve the remains and piece them back together again, or, like a virus, it can spread quietly through your soul, decoding and recoding your cells until it abruptly stops and pulls the plug and you watch in horror as your life disappears from beneath your feet.

Alex carried the kind of pain that destroys one's soul. He could hear the sucking sound as his spirit drained from him, and he frantically searched for the plug. He had carried his past like a heavy burden, dragging the memories behind him. He feared baring his wounded soul to the world.

Sometimes the healing can only begin when the life-sucking demons of the past are confronted, and the hunted becomes the dragon slayer and claims victory over his life.

In a sequence of stolen moments, it was to be a weekend of revelation and transformation.

Alex and Claudia sat opposite each other at Claudia's favourite pizzeria. It had been Gareth's favourite pizzeria, too. Claudia knew that she was taking a huge personal risk being in a public place with Alex, but it was dark, and they were sitting outside, and this minimised the chances of anyone seeing them.

At one point, they noticed the waiters packing the chairs on to the tables and switching the restaurant lights off.

It was agreed that Claudia and Alex could stay. "Just leave your wine glasses on the table when you leave," the waiter said, smiling from ear to ear.

Tell me about your father, Alex, Claudia ventured, tipsy from the sangria but strangely present. "Tell me why you had that fall out all those years ago."

Alex shuffled in his chair, "Do you really want to go there?" he asked. "I'm not even sure that *I* want to go there,"

"It's important to me, Alex, but if you're not ready to talk about that part of your life, I won't force you to."

Alex stood up, walked around the table, and sat down next to her.

"I had just finished my term in the army, and it was my first day out. I was so happy to be going home. I couldn't wait to see my family."

He sighed and continued. "I had a strong urge to see my father because our relationship had been rather unsteady over the years, and I guess that the army, as much as it toughens a person up, also makes us realise what is really important."

Claudia took Alex's hand and threaded her fingers among his.

"So I asked my mother to take me to him. They were separated at that stage, but she had his address. I could not wait to see him, man to man."

"I arrived at my father's apartment and knocked on the door," he continued. "I was so excited to be there."

Claudia smiled and squeezed his hand.

"But when my father opened the door, he was not happy to see me. In fact, his response was one of disdain, as if I had inconvenienced him by being there. I told him that I had just finished my time in the army and that I really wanted to spend some time with him. He looked at me and said, "Alex, I don't have the time to spend with you right now." Then, he promptly closed the door in my face. I just stood there, dumbfounded. My own father had turned me away. I lifted my hand to knock on the door again, to try to get through to him one more time, but I didn't have the courage. In the end, I just turned around and walked away."

"Did he ever try to reach you after that?" Claudia asked, confused.

"Nope. In fact, that was the last time I saw him. He moved from that apartment and left no forwarding address. To this day, I have no idea whether he is dead or alive."

Claudia watched as Alex's eyes filled with tears. They tumbled out and rolled down his cheeks. "I have always felt so empty inside ever since," he said, fighting back the tears. "My father rejected me. And every boy needs his dad. It doesn't matter whether you're a little boy or a grown man – it is still the same. After what he did, as far as I was concerned, he might as well have been dead."

Claudia felt a lump in her throat and wiped the tears from her eyes, "That must have destroyed you, Alex."

"I guess it did," he said, smiling sadly. "All I ever wanted was to have that father and son bond that so many of my friends shared with their fathers."

"That is so sad. Did you ever try to track him down again after that?"

"I did, many times, in fact. Christine had a friend in the police, and they managed to locate him in several different places. But he had always moved on. He was like a gypsy – every lead was a dead end. After a while, there were no more leads. That's when I presumed that he had either left the country or that he was dead. Either way, I knew that I would never see him again."

"And his family? Surely there must be someone who might have stayed in contact with him?" asked Claudia.

"I never knew his family," said Alex and sighed. "All I know is that they lived in Wales, but nothing more than that. I wouldn't even know where to start."

"Do you think that he might be in Wales?" Claudia asked hopefully.

"Maybe," said Alex. "But honestly, there have been so many dead ends that this would probably end up being another one of them."

"Maybe we should fly to Wales and hunt him down," Claudia smiled teasingly.

"I don't think he wants to be found," said Alex.

∽

It must have been around midnight when they finally left the restaurant. Claudia could feel a deeper bond of trust had been forged between them. For the first time in weeks, she felt as if she was truly connecting with Alex. He was finally letting her inside the deep, dark crevices of a heart that had spent more years than he could remember trying to protect from being broken. His mother, his father, his many failed relationships, Christine and her affairs, the list seemed endless.

"I promise you with every fibre of my being, Alex," said Claudia, looking him directly in the eyes, "I will never, ever betray you, and I will never break your heart."

Alex smiled and hugged her tightly. There were no words to be said. He wanted to believe her more than anything. But he could not utter the words, "I know". Not yet.

The road was dark, and their emotions were high. Alex placed one hand on the steering wheel, and the other was wrapped around Claudia's shoulders. He turned towards her and smiled. He loved her with all his heart.

"Alex, STOP!" screamed Claudia, pressing her hands down on the dashboard. Alex quickly turned to face the road, and he felt his foot plunge down onto the brakes as a young fawn stood in the middle of the road, its eyes locked on the car's headlights.

"No!" cried Claudia as she felt the thud. It was too late.

Claudia and Alex turned around. The little body lay in the middle of the road, lifeless and still. Alex reversed the car and parked it in the dirt on the side of the road. Claudia was crying uncontrollably. She knelt down next to the fawn and touched his face. He was still warm. He was still alive. His breathing was laboured, the little nostrils on his velvet nose were flared, and his eyes were glazed over. Alex crouched down next to her and put his arm around her shoulders.

"I'm so sorry, Claudia."

They watched as the fawn took his last few breaths. There was nothing they could do to save him. Blood ran from his mouth and on to the road, glinting off the moonlight. Claudia felt ill. She took her hand and gently closed his eyes.

"I'm so sorry, little one," she said. "I'm so very sorry."

Alex took the fawn by his hind legs and pulled him out of the road. His mother was still standing on the side of the road, waiting patiently for her baby to cross the road after her.

Alex and Claudia stood together in silence, the shock and the sorrow at the precious little life that they had unwittingly snuffed out, tearing through their souls. Here today, gone tomorrow.

How precious the fleeting passage of time is, Claudia thought.

∞

"I'll challenge you to a game of squash if you're keen," grinned Alex as he poured Claudia a tall glass of orange juice over breakfast.

"Challenge accepted," laughed Claudia. "In fact, prepare to have your ass whipped!"

Raucous laughter erupted from the squash court as they whizzed past each other.

"Ten all!" shouted Alex, planting a kiss on Claudia's forehead as he retrieved the ball and sent it hurtling back across the wall, his shoes squeaking against the floor.

"Eleven to me!" laughed Claudia as he missed the shot, the ball rolling across the court.

"You're one hell of a player," grinned Alex, mopping the beads of perspiration from his forehead and plonking himself down on the floor. "I think I've just had my ass well and properly whipped. By a girl, too!"

"I warned you that you'd met your match," said Claudia, beaming. "Ready for another round?"

∞

Being a whisky connoisseur, Alex introduced Claudia to a fine single malt Scottish whisky over lunch, and they whiled away the few precious hours that they had left together before Claudia returned home to her children, who had spent the day with Grace and Charlie.

Alex shared intimate details of his childhood with Claudia, his soul raw and exposed as he relived the harrowing memories of growing up in a home wrecked by the insidious abuse of alcohol. When his mother drank, she often became belligerent and angry and sometimes physically attacked Alex and his brother, with Alex often bearing the brunt of her violent outbursts.

"There were times when I would curl myself into a ball and huddle in a corner while she hurled her abuse at me," said Alex sadly. "It would go on like that for hours. She would blame me for everything that was wrong in her life. Everything."

Claudia thought back to Gareth's father, a kind, gentle man who transformed into a psychopathic demon when his lips touched the bottle. She cringed as she remembered watching many a beautiful day turn into a frightening nightmare as his temper flared and the full wrath of his insecurities were unearthed onto his family as the alcohol resurrected his courage and turned him into a monster.

She struggled to imagine what it must have been like for Alex to have to endure such abuse as a young boy.

"I really struggle to connect with her now," said Alex. "As I mentioned to you before, when we talk, it's always the alcohol talking back to me. Her sober moments are few and far between, and when she calls me, I never really know what to expect."

"It's such a pity that she doesn't realise how much of a rift she has built between the two of you," said Claudia. "I really hope that she comes to her senses one day. She's missing out on so much."

"I know," said Alex despondently. "I hope she realises its impact before it's too late."

"You have to realise that alcoholism is a disease, Alex," said Claudia. "And she is the only person who can free herself from it. She has to be the one to take the first step."

"She doesn't see that," said Alex. "And as much as I try to restrain myself, the second I hear the alcohol breathing down the line, the hairs on the back of my neck stand up, and I find myself switching off. She really brings out the worst in me."

"Sometimes we need to be kind," said Claudia gently. "She is probably fighting battles within herself that you know nothing about. The alcohol is probably the only thing that drowns the pain out. Rather than getting your back up next time she calls, you should try to be gentler. Perhaps then she will show you her softer side. We all mirror each other in one way or another, you know."

"You're right," said Alex. "I guess I cannot build anything with her if I keep breaking her down."

"Exactly. And as far as you know, she's all you have left. If she knows she is loved, she might show you another side of her soul."

"Thank you, my darling," said Alex warmly. "I'm going to make a concerted effort to hold my tongue next time."

∽

Letting in and letting go. The butterfly that is trapped between our hands will flutter instinctively as it struggles to break free. The heartbreak of abandonment, the trauma of abuse, the gut-wrenching torment and humiliation of betrayal; each one holds the power to either crush us or ultimately free us. Alex and Christine's divorce was waiting in the wings, preparing to make its grand entrance on to the stage of their shattered lives. Alex was plagued with feelings of inadequacy and powerlessness, deeply ashamed that he had failed in a contract as sacred as marriage. The hands that were holding his life were opening, and he could see the light streaming in, yet still, he was terrified of what might be waiting for him on the other side. Where would he go? How would he cope? Could he fight this beast alone?

Sometimes, life has us backed up against the wall. The wolves are gnashing their teeth against the door to our hearts, digging under the foundations of everything that we hold dear, waiting for that weak spot to appear so that they can tear through it and rip it to shreds. There is a legend told by the Native American Indians of the two wolves that live within us, one being angry and bitter and resentful and the other filled with peace and love and joy. The wolves battle it out against each other, and sooner or later, one triumphs over the other. In the end, the wolf that wins is the one we feed.

It is so sad, thought Claudia, that so many people spend so much time feeding the wolf that is trying to destroy them.

It was late. Kyle and Ross were fast asleep, and Claudia was alone. Thinking back on the events of the day, she wrote to Alex.

October 10th, 18:40 pm

Claudia Stevenson

Alex, my heart broke when you shared the intimate details of your tormented childhood with me. You have always told me that you avoid confrontation, and it occurred to me that perhaps – resting deeply in your subconscious mind – you were so profoundly affected by what happened in your past that it has always just been easier to place other people's feelings before your own.

We are not here to wage war against the world. Instead, we are here to build bridges. We are not here to harbour grudges and resentment towards others. We are here to build a foundation of mutual respect, acceptance, compromise, and trust. What I really, really realised is how good we are together, a formidable team – a match made in heaven.

I know this bothers you, but please believe me when I say that there is absolutely nothing wrong with you for showing me "your weaker side", as you put it. It is so powerful when you are able to really feel things on a deep emotional level.

I know that you are feeling completely overwhelmed right now, and we are all entitled to feel this way from time to time. It often hits us out of left field, leaving us with very little time to digest or even understand what is going on.

Please don't feel that you have to put up a front with me because I want to see all of you. I want to experience your happiness, your sadness, your successes and your frustrations. Most importantly, and especially right now, I want to be there for you in the same way that you were there for me.

You have no idea how much you helped me deal with all of my pain and frustration when I felt that everything was crashing down on me, that there was so much to do, so many people demanding my time, not being the efficient and organised (and most importantly "in control") person that I always was. I often wanted to shut myself off from the world and not deal with any of it, wishing that I could fast forward that darn clock to a time in the future when all of this was behind me.

The past two months have been fraught with turmoil and upheaval, but I realised that the more I ticked off the boxes on my to-do list and the more people I entrusted to help me, the easier things became. I know that my focus on my business is not at one hundred percent yet, but I am refusing to put too much pressure on myself because I know how unproductive I am when I am feeling overwhelmed. If the boys have to eat takeaways for the next month, then so be it. If I have to work every night until the end of the year, then so be it. If I don't return personal calls immediately, I'm not going to beat myself up about it. I'll get there. If I can't do something, I say so. Nobody knows what it's like unless they've experienced a huge shift in their lives like we have. We can't expect people to understand, but at least we can be honest and stop bending over backwards for them. Just admitting to myself that I need time out was a step in the right direction.

The most important thing I learned was how having support can help us rise above anything. My friends have been amazing. I have taken them up on their offers to help me because it helped me cope. They know that if they were ever in the same situation, I would do exactly the same for them.

But the most incredible love and support that I have received has been from you, my angel. Knowing that there was a light at the end of this very long and sometimes very dark tunnel was my inspiration through all of this. A more honest and understanding person I could not have asked for, and I truly love you for that.

All I want you to know is that I understand what you are going through right now (and I really mean that) – I feel your sadness, I sense your frustration, but I also know how much strength you have, and I know that once you start dealing with all of the things you have to get through, you are going to start feeling even stronger.

I really love you, and I cannot wait for all of this to be over for you because it's just so amazing when you start feeling that your life is getting back on track.

October 10th, 21:48 pm

Alex Winterton

Thank you so much for this beautiful message. I love you so much.

I really want to seem strong, you know, it's what I have to do every day to the entire world – customers, staff, partners, friends – and I guess after a while, I forget how I am actually feeling, thinking I am so strong that I can handle anything until finally, uncontrollably, the whole thing just comes crashing down.

Thank you for allowing me to be me and not somebody that everybody expects me to be – this really means the world to me.

I am so glad that I have been there for you and that I was really able to help you through this. I am glad that I was your guiding light and a beacon of hope for you. In the same way, you are that beacon for me now.

As for the road ahead, you are right. I know that once this is behind me, nothing will stop me, you and us. We have so much ahead of us, so much potential, so much excitement, and so much to create.

Thank you to the Universe, for you. Thank you to you, for us.

PHILLIPA MITCHELL

Thank you, thank you, thank you, thank you!
I love you, darling.

CHAPTER 21

Claudia checked her speedometer. It read one hundred and seventy kilometres per hour. She was travelling in an eighty zone. On a euphoric high, Claudia was on her way to meet Alex, and were it not for fear of incarceration, she would have stepped down harder on the pedal.

Alex was standing outside the house waiting for her, catching raindrops on his tongue. The thunder rumbled in the distance, and Claudia walked up to him with her arms outstretched. They hugged and kissed and breathed into each other, savouring their precious moment in time.

How Claudia wished that the world would stop turning, just for a few days. Soon, Alex would be driving off into the distance again, and she could feel the pain of separation tearing through her heart.

"I've reserved a table for us at our favourite spot," said Alex. "Let's hope that they leave the lights on for us this time."

Claudia smiled. "I cannot wait," she said. "I'm famished."

Sitting across the table from each other, Claudia heard the familiar words to Elton John's song *Sacrifice* playing in the background; the song they had danced to seventeen years before when they were living their separate lives when they were two hearts living in two separate worlds, yet both longing to be together.

Claudia could feel the tears welling in her eyes. She remembered that night as if it were yesterday. She remembered how Alex had held her, how she had pulled herself close to him, how she had wished the song would never end. She had listened to the irony of the words, knowing that he had moved on. But she had not. She could not. She thought he was gone forever.

"Are you okay, my darling?" Alex asked, pulling her towards him.

"I'm sorry, Alex, it's just this song. It's the song that played at that Christmas party all those years ago when I thought I had lost you forever. I honestly have to pinch myself every time I think about where we find ourselves now. I'm listening to the song, and I am thinking to myself that the word 'sacrifice' is so true when I look back on our story. I never knew it then, but it hurts like hell right now."

"How so?" he asked.

"It's like the Universe is a giant chessboard. The pieces are being moved around the board by a grand master. Sometimes, the threat of attack is stronger than the execution, and sometimes, the execution of that threat is where the game finally ends. Gareth threatened me with divorce in an attempt to nudge me in a certain direction, but he was actually just testing me. He did not expect me to make a move. And it was that move that resulted in the ultimate sacrifice: the sacrifice of his life for mine."

Alex put his arms around her, "You're right," he said softly, "and it's so sad when you look at it that way. I will forever be grateful to Gareth for letting me capture his queen."

Claudia smiled, "I would have preferred all the pieces to have remained on the board, Alex – it is the casualties of the choices we make that haunt us the most in life."

༄

It was Saturday morning and the dawn of the Rugby World Cup final: England against South Africa. Grace and Charlie had invited Claudia and Alex over to their place to watch the game. They would be meeting Alex for the first time.

"It feels as if we're coming out of hiding," laughed Claudia as she pulled her green and gold rugby shirt over her head.

"Not if I have anything to say about it," teased Alex, holding her arms up and kissing her on her belly as she pleaded with him to release her.

Flushed and giggling, Claudia finally pulled her head through the top of her shirt.

"If you don't stop that, we're really going to be late," she laughed.

Before she could say another word, Alex had removed her shirt, and Claudia could hear the world humming quietly in the distance as he gently lay her down on the bed, his lips touching hers, the heat of his body as she felt him inside her…

Claudia felt an incredible amount of pride emanating from her heart as she introduced Alex to Grace and Charlie. Grace winked at Claudia, mouthing the words "Ooh la la!"

Claudia grinned and winked back at her.

What an evening it turned out to be: South Africa won the game for the first time in twelve years. Claudia remembered watching South Africa win the game with Gareth back in 1995. They were newlyweds at the time and had no idea of the path that lay ahead of them. So much can happen in twelve years, Claudia thought to herself. If somebody had told her twelve years ago that she would be sharing her life with Alex twelve years down the line, she would have laughed them off.

October 21st, 22:31 pm

Claudia Stevenson

Sometimes, love is unexpected, and sometimes it is unpredictable.

Have I ever been in love? Yes, I have, and it was seventeen years ago...

During the time that we were apart, there was love, but it was a different kind of love. Not the love that shooting stars and moon dust are made of...

Did I ever think I'd find love again in this lifetime? Not in my wildest dreams...

Am I in love right now? Without a doubt...!

My darling, if I have ever been sure of us and more in love with you, this weekend was it. How I love and cherish what we have found in each other.

I love you, and I miss you, and it hurts like hell having to wave goodbye to you every time you leave.

October 21st, 23:14 pm

Alex Winterton

My darling,

I am not a poet or a songwriter, but one thing I know for sure is how much I love you.

I know how time speeds up when we are together. I know how I feel when you kiss me and how your touch reverberates through my soul.

You have made my heart lighter and my world so much brighter.

I am truly blessed to have found you.

As the days moved into weeks, Claudia could feel a sense of normality returning to her life. She felt stronger and more independent, and she was breathing easier. The perfect storm that she had been trapped in for more than two months since Gareth passed away was levelling out. The rain had stopped falling, and the clouds were making space for the sun to shine through again.

The hurt and the guilt never really left her, but the heavy weight that had shrouded her was lifting.

For Alex, his journey was only beginning. His mind was made up, but he continued to return home to his estranged wife and everything that comprised his double life.

Claudia could not understand the reasons for his procrastination. Christine had cheated on him, for God's sake. And not just once but multiple times. Claudia was waiting for Alex with open arms, and yet he continued to insist that he needed more time. Time for what?

"Claudia," said Alex anxiously. "I feel as if you're rushing me to move on, and you're right – I do need to move on, but I need to take this a little slower. There are other people involved in this equation, and it's important that I think about them, too. I can't just get up and walk out. There is a process that I have to follow."

"Alex, if you continue to hold on like this, you're never going to be able to release yourself from this marriage," protested Claudia. "Either you want to stay or you want to go. You're sitting on the fence right now. Don't get me wrong, but I think I'm right when I say you're practising double standards."

"I'm not practising double standards, Claudia – well, at least I don't think I am," said Alex, taking her by the hand. " But I can promise you that I am going to start taking the steps I need to take to move on in my life so that we can be together."

Claudia sighed. "I hope you don't think I'm being selfish. I know you need to sort your life out, and I understand that this is a difficult time for you. It just hurts that we have this moment in time that has opened up for us to be together, and you're continuously pulling up the handbrake."

"You are in no way being selfish," said Alex. "I know you're fighting for the things you want. I understand and appreciate this completely."

"Why are you so concerned about how Christine is going to cope with you leaving, Alex? She is the one who asked for a divorce, not you. Surely the natural thing for you to do now is to move out and move on with your life?"

Alex leaned forward and looked Claudia in the eyes for what felt like an eternity.

"Christine does not have a hold over me. You must remember that we have been together for nine years. I can't simply stop considering her feelings. I don't want to sound like a martyr, but I do want to tread lightly. Also, I am extremely sensitive to my stepdaughters' feelings. So it is with all of this in mind that I am being extra cautious."

Claudia thought about how she had agreed to allow Kyle and Ross to stay overnight at Gareth's parents' the following Friday night. Alex had asked to see her, and she had placed her needs above those of her children so that she could spend one precious night with him. Only to be told two days later that he had changed his mind – that he thought it would be more honourable to spend a weekend at home with Christine so that he would not be forced to answer her prying questions about where he had been – and with whom.

"Alex, I went against my better judgement when Gareth's parents asked to have the boys on Friday night. Perhaps you should try considering my feelings and those of Kyle and Ross before you consider those of the person who has hardly given any thought to yours."

"I'm sorry, Claudia," said Alex, "That was wrong of me, I know. If you can just give me some time to make a clean break from Christine, I promise you that we will have our chance to be together.

All I want is to be able to give you what you need and deserve."

"I still don't understand why you still feel that you have to answer to her," said Claudia, confused. "She is making the process so difficult for you even though she was the one who betrayed you in the first place. It makes no sense."

"Claudia, you are three steps ahead of me right now, possibly even more," said Alex dejectedly. "I am just trying to deal with this in the best way I know how. The pain I am feeling at the moment is unbearable, and I am really struggling to keep everything clear in my mind."

"I know," sighed Claudia. "I wish that we could fast forward the clock and put all of this behind us. I wish we were on the same page. I guess I just need to realise that the sacrifices we are both making at the moment pale in comparison to what we are going to gain in the long term."

"Thank you, Claudia," said Alex, fighting back the tears. "I really appreciate your willingness to give me the space I need. I am so sorry for upsetting you, especially about Friday night. I promise you that I am going to put some real effort into being clearer with you in future."

Navigating his ship through the churning waves of emotions that flooded the ocean of his soul, his eyes burning from the salty spray, his knuckles white, and his stomach knotted with fear, Alex knew that he would have to hold on to the wheel with every ounce of strength that he possessed in order to steer his vessel safely through the rough seas. It was time for him to batten down the hatches and for Claudia to pray with all her might that they would hold.

∾

Every so often, as we hurtle down the highway of life, we fail to notice the complexities of the journeys of those with whom we share the road. We may have passed through our dark tunnels, but there are others who are accelerating towards their own. Claudia felt a gloomy cloud of sadness descending over her. Her tunnel had been dark and cold, but Alex had taken her by the hand and guided her through the shadows. She had burst out on the other side, and she was ready to start living again.

Claudia felt awful. Selfish. Her intentions had always been pure. She knew that she was rushing Alex, but it was only because she yearned for them to be together without him having to answer to Christine and without her having to make excuses to her children. She realised that even though she had needed Alex to walk beside her as she took her first tentative steps into her new life, perhaps he did not need the same from her. She knew that she had to respect that and give him the space to extricate himself from his past without the overshadowing fear of reprisal that he feared from Christine.

It was time to take a step back and focus on the present. As much as Alex was consuming every part of her existence, she had to concentrate on maintaining her sanity and providing a safe harbour for her children. She had to drop the anchor and secure her own ship before she drifted off into an ocean of uncertainty.

༄

It was the 30th of October, and Ross was celebrating his seventh birthday – his first birthday without his father. Claudia was overcompensating hopelessly.

"Will I be getting a new dad for my birthday?" Ross asked, his eyes twinkling.

Lynne, the boy's play therapist, had told Claudia the day before that, in her professional opinion, the time was right for Claudia to introduce the children to Alex.

Claudia had planned a birthday party for Ross that Sunday, and Alex had proposed that they use the opportunity to remove the chains that bound them to their old lives and step out from behind the curtains and on to the stage that formed the foundation for their new life together.

"Let's wait and see, my darling," Claudia said, kissing him on the forehead and ruffling his hair. "Let's just wait and see."

꩜

"Guess what?" said Alex down the other end of the telephone line.

"I'm curious, tell me?" asked Claudia, wondering what he was about to share with her.

"I've found a place, I've signed the lease, and I'm moving in this weekend," he said, smiling, wishing that he could see the expression on her face.

"Are you being serious?" Claudia asked, "Seriously serious?"

"Seriously serious," he replied.

"Do you know that you have literally just blown my mind?" she said, wanting to scream with delight, wishing that he was there so that she could hug him and kiss him and hold him tight. "I cannot believe this!"

"Well, believe it, girl. No more Mr. Procrastinator for me. Now it's time for Mr. Action to take control."

"I'm so proud of you," said Claudia.

"Christine will be away this weekend, so the timing is perfect. I have already told her that she will be coming home to an empty house. I can move in on Saturday and wake up fresh on Sunday morning for Ross' birthday party."

"You're amazing, Alex, do you know that?" said Claudia as she leaned back in her chair. "How did Christine receive the news?"

"She was in tears," said Alex. "I think that it all hit home for her today. I don't think she ever expected me to be so emotionally strong about letting her go. And I have you to thank for that."

∽

And so, within a matter of days, Alex was finally *home*. As he turned the key in the lock to the door of his new apartment, he closed one chapter of his life and opened a brand new one. As they sat outside on the balcony later that afternoon, Claudia watched months, if not years, of tension and anxiety lift from him.

"I cannot believe how liberating this feels, Claudia," he said, putting his arm around her shoulders, "I spent so many years living somebody else's life that I think I overlooked what I really wanted. I had almost forgotten who I was."

"I'm incredibly proud of you," Claudia said as she watched the sun slowly setting, painting the sky a deep orange and pink. "Today is the first day of your new life. Now you can leave your past exactly where it belongs: in the past."

Alex smiled. "Exactly. From now on, it's you and me against the world."

∞

Arriving at the party venue, Claudia rushed to unpack everything and lay the table before the guests arrived. Alex had planned to arrive early to meet the boys, and Claudia's heart was pounding with anticipation. Would the boys accept Alex? Would he accept them?

"I really hope that Alex is going to be there today," said Kyle.

"Me too," said Ross. "It would be the best birthday present ever."

"I'm not making any promises," said Claudia warmly. "Let's just wait and see."

"I know he is going to be here today," said Kyle. "I can feel it in my bones."

Claudia winked at him and whispered in his ear – "Well, let's keep this a surprise for your brother then."

Kyle grinned uncontrollably and skipped around the table. "Today is going to be the best day ever, Ross!"

Ross laughed and chased him back around the table.

"Come over here, you two," called Claudia. "I need two big pairs of lungs to blow all of these balloons up."

Kyle insisted on waiting downstairs in the hope that he would see Alex arrive. To his absolute delight, Alex parked almost directly in front of him, and he knew immediately that it was Alex. Claudia watched as Alex walked towards Kyle and offered him a handshake. Her heart was singing as Kyle rushed up the stairs, grinning like a Cheshire cat and announcing that Alex had arrived.

After greeting Claudia with a brief kiss hello, Alex walked over to Ross and knelt down next to him.

"Happy birthday, Ross," he said and smiled, Ross beaming back at him shyly. "I'm Alex."

"Hello, Alex," said Ross in a small voice. "Are you here for my birthday party?"

"I am," said Alex warmly. " I wouldn't have missed it for the world. I've got something in my car for you. Would you like to come downstairs with me and see what it is?"

Alex reached down for Ross' hand, and Ross immediately slipped his little hand into his. They walked down the stairs together. As they walked away, Ross turned around and looked at Claudia, his eyes bright with excitement.

Within a matter of minutes, Ross dashed back upstairs carrying a huge, brightly wrapped box. He tore away the paper and screamed with excitement when he saw the gift inside.

"It's a Transformer, Mommy! This is so cool!"

Alex smiled at Claudia, and she felt her heart melting inside. She squeezed Alex's hand and mouthed the words "Thank you" to him.

The venue was an indoor snow centre complete with skis, tubes, and bum boards, and the children laughed hysterically as they zoomed down the slopes. While Alex busied himself taking photographs of the celebrations, Ross put his arms around Claudia.

"Mommy, he is so kind."

"Come here, guys!" shouted Alex above the noise, waving four plastic bum boards in the air. "Let's make a train and go down the slope together!"

Kyle and Ross ran towards him excitedly, grabbing the bum boards from his hands. As they hurtled down the slope, Alex veered off towards the side, and they hit the barriers, squashing each other and falling in a tumbled heap at the bottom, everyone roaring with laughter.

"Let's do it again, Alex," giggled Kyle, grabbing Alex by the hand and pulling him up off the floor.

"Yes, please, Alex," begged Ross, pulling on Alex's arm. "But I want to be in the front this time!"

"Well, let's get this train out of the station then," laughed Alex as they held on to each other, the snow spraying out from beneath them.

"Can Alex come home with us, Mommy?" pleaded Ross when the party was over. Kyle was nodding his head at Claudia fervently.

Claudia glanced at Alex, and Alex nodded back at her.

"Besides, somebody has got to help you build that transformer," he said, winking at Ross.

Whooping with delight, Ross leapt into Alex's car while Claudia loaded Ross' gifts into the back of her car.

"Shotgun, I'm going with Alex," he declared, fastening his seatbelt.

"Alright then, my boy," said Claudia, laughing. "Kyle will keep me company then."

Kyle could hardly contain his excitement as he drove home with Claudia that afternoon. "Mom, Alex is so much fun! I really like him a lot," he said. "And we have so much in common."

It was as if Kyle was trying to find something, anything, that he could use to identify himself with Alex and make Alex feel as if he were a part of him – that the void that Gareth had left in his life could be closed.

"Mom, do you think that you will marry Alex so that we can be a real family again?" he asked.

"Let's take one day at a time, my boy," Claudia said cautiously, wanting nothing more than to stand before the altar with her childhood sweetheart and promise to share her life with him. "I don't want to rush anything. I think we owe that to Dad, don't you?"

Kyle nodded silently. "I just really like him, Mom."

Later that evening, as Claudia, Kyle and Ross stood on the veranda, waving goodbye to Alex as he drove away from the house, Ross hugged Claudia.

"Mommy, he really is so kind".

Claudia smiled, a feeling of peace enveloping her. "I'm so happy that you like Alex, my darling."

"Mommy, do you know that I actually received two presents from Alex today?"

"Two presents?" Claudia mused. "I definitely saw one present. What was the second one?"

"The second present was Alex."

CHAPTER 22

Two and a half years later

Like a man dragging his body through the desert, gasping, dehydrated and weak, the soul will continue to seek out its oasis. Closure is the sustenance the human condition craves to drown out the parched trappings of the troubled conscience.

Increasingly desperate to find the answers that would not come to her through logical deduction, Claudia sought out the advice of a spiritual life coach to exorcise the demons of guilt and confusion that continued to haunt her.

It was not just Gareth – it was everything: her business, her relationship with Alex, her children... It was as if everything was interconnected by a web of uncertainty, and Claudia needed answers.

As much as she tried to forget Gareth, he was always there, and Claudia knew that she would be unable to rest until she was certain that his soul was at peace.

Her business was struggling. Claudia was watching it collapse before her eyes as it haemorrhaged cash to the point where she had begun selling off her insurance policies, her life savings, her children's university education funds – anything she could lay her hands on to pay the bills. In tears, she had fallen to her knees in front of the principal at Ross and Kyle's school, begging him to keep the children enrolled despite the fact that she was months behind with their fees. She often felt as if her life had been cursed when Gareth died, that he was punishing her from another realm.

And, as far as Alex was concerned, Claudia waited with earnest expectation for the day that Alex would, on bended knee, ask for her hand in marriage. She longed to put her past behind her and feel as if she were part of something greater with Alex, acutely aware of the sanctity and security that such a union would bring. She eventually began to lose count of the special occasions and what seemed to be carefully planned holidays in yet another exotic location that were simply special occasions and holidays in exotic destinations. She dared not bring the subject up for fear of chasing him away. She was already losing her grip on everything else in her life. She could not afford to lose Alex in the process.

The mystical fragrance of the sandalwood incense wisped its way through the room. Claudia felt the warmth of the sun's rays as they settled upon her lap. She shivered and breathed out deeply. This was it, she thought – her moment of truth.

"Just relax and take a few deep breaths," the woman said soothingly. "Clear your mind."

A few silent minutes passed between them.

"You are afraid," she observed. "And you don't like yourself much either, do you?"

Claudia smiled weakly, "Oh boy," she thought. "Here we go."

"This man you live with," she said, "you love him very much, don't you?"

Claudia nodded.

"He is very much in love with you, Claudia," she continued, "but I sense that he is blocking you from the light."

Claudia rubbed her hands together, feeling a chill run down her spine.

"You are a very strong, spiritual woman, and he is a good, solid person on the outside. But on the inside..." she sighed, "on the inside, he is a fragile person. His vulnerability is making him want to shield you from his fragility."

Claudia swallowed hard and forced her eyes shut.

"Sometimes you are just downright afraid. And so is he. Claudia, what is his name?"

"It's Alex," Claudia said softly.

"Alex is scared, too, but he cannot admit to it. He is trying to overcompensate. He grew up in a house where a lot was expected of him, and he put so much pressure on himself. In his mind, he was never good enough. He always thought he was failing."

Claudia fought back the tears. How could this woman know so much about Alex?

"You don't believe that you are good enough either, Claudia," she said. "You are always measuring yourself up against others."

Claudia thought about how she had begun to feel that she was not good enough for Alex. Her hopes and dreams seemed so distant from his. Claudia's dreams were about family and togetherness, and his had become about money and power.

"He would make an excellent father," the woman said, "but there is definitely a baby issue. He has this conception that all successful people should father a child. And he has not fathered a child, has he?"

Claudia shook her head. "He has never really mentioned starting a family. It has always been a point of contention between us because I would want more than anything else to be his wife and to have his child, a little being that we have created together, a symbol of our love for each other. But he always brushes me off when I bring it up, so I don't mention it any more. I've just put the subject to the side."

"Your business too, Claudia," she continued, "you need to find stability within yourself if you want your business and your personal life to be more stable. Your hard times are not over yet."

The room was silent, and Claudia listened to the birds singing outside.

"You were married before, weren't you?" she asked.

Claudia sat up in her chair. "Yes, I was."

"But he is not here any more, is he?"

"No, he's not," Claudia replied.

"Did he die in a car accident?"

Claudia nodded and wrung her hands together.

"He is here, Claudia. He is here in this room with us right now. He is holding a big bunch of yellow roses. They are for you."

Claudia felt her heartbeat quicken. She had never witnessed a soul being channelled before, and she felt the hairs on the back of her neck standing up straight. She was fearful of Gareth's resentment towards her and was unsure as to whether he had carried it with him into the spiritual realm.

"He is telling me that he feels so guilty that he left you with the children. He is saying that he is extremely worried about his parents. He doesn't think that they have ever got over his death."

Claudia sighed. She knew that his parents were struggling to cope and move on without him, even after all this time.

"He says that he could have stayed, but things went horribly wrong," she continued. "He did not intend to die that day."

Claudia felt her blood draining out of her body. Her hands were ice cold.

"He wanted to be your knight in shining armour again, Claudia," the woman said. "He thought that by having an accident and hurting himself, you would run to his side to take care of him, that you would beg him to take you back."

"But it didn't work out that way," whispered Claudia, reliving the night of his death, the phone calls, the music, his words when he said that he would never take her back. There was so much hatred in those memories.

"But it all went horribly wrong," the woman continued. "He realised in those final moments that he had gone too far."

The room fell silent.

"He is not angry with you, Claudia," the woman said. "He keeps telling me that he is not angry with you."

Claudia swallowed and tried to catch the tear that ran down her cheek.

"He is still very Earthbound," she continued. "Your oldest son – the tall boy with the sandy hair – can sometimes see and feel his father. He is saying that he is still here because he wants to be here for his children."

"He's smiling at you, Claudia," she said gently. "And he is holding the roses out to you. He is saying thank you for holding his name so high with the children and for never saying anything bad about him to them. He is very grateful for this."

Claudia sobbed. "Please tell him how sorry I am, too," she said. "I never wanted him to leave like this. I never wanted him to die. I feel so wretched about what I did to him."

"He is at peace now," the woman said. "And he needs you to believe that."

Claudia nodded her head. "I really want to believe that."

The room was quiet.

"He has gone now, Claudia."

"Thank you for channelling him," said Claudia, deeply grateful. "I was not expecting him to come through. I really believed that he had too much hatred for me to show himself to me."

"When we leave this Earth," the woman explained, "we leave all that baggage behind. There is only peace and love and light. Everything makes sense on the other side."

"His parents," she continued, "your husband is right – they have never come to terms with his death."

Claudia nodded. "They despise me so much, I don't think they would want to hear the truth from me. All they see me as is the person who took their son away from them."

The woman reached her hand out to Claudia. "Have you got any plans for the rest of the day?" she asked.

"I was going to go back to the office," Claudia replied.

"I think you should be gentle on yourself today," she said warmly. "In fact, I am going to recommend that you leave here today, go and buy yourself a notepad and a pen, and I want you to write to your husband's parents. I want you to open your heart to them. Even if they never forgive you, at least you will know that you have reached out to them. And then I want you to mail that letter to them."

Claudia smiled. "Okay, I think I can do that. I think this is exactly what I need to do."

They hugged each other goodbye, and Claudia sat quietly in her car for a few moments, allowing the moment to flood through her body. Her heart was breaking for Gareth. She thought about Alex and how he fitted into the giant puzzle of her life. She had to find a way to get through to him. She knew that if she failed to realise her dream with Alex, Gareth's death would have been meaningless. She did not think that she could live with herself if she couldn't see this one through to the end.

Claudia drove into the country and parked alongside a beautiful river. There was not a soul around. She pulled out the notepad and pen and began to write…

Dear Mom and Dad,

It has taken me a long time to put pen to paper and write to you, but the time feels right, and I would like to ask you to put your feelings about me aside and listen to what I have to share with you.

The day and night of Gareth's death has haunted me for longer than I can remember. So many unanswered questions, so much hurt, so much anger, and so much pain. I have felt so completely emp-

ty, so responsible, and so unable to deal with what happened. I have felt so disconnected from reality, wishing that there was some way that I could have done things differently, wanting so desperately to be able to turn back the clock and change things, yet knowing all along that nothing I can do or say would ever bring him back.

I tried for more years than I can remember to love and understand Gareth more. I wanted our marriage to work so badly and for us to find peace with each other. Gareth had become so depressed and so angry with life and everything in it. His only way of making himself feel better was by buying "stuff", yet it never seemed to fill what was missing in his life. He became critical and judgemental. It was so difficult to talk to him and have a normal relationship.

I longed for more, but I felt as if there was a brick wall between the two of us. I went for counselling, I tried to speak to him, and often, just for a while, he would go back to being the old Gareth that I knew. There were a few days of happiness, but then life got *to him again, and he became sad and withdrawn and nothing I said or did made him feel better.*

The day he died so tragically was the day my world fell apart. He asked for a divorce in the middle of an argument, and I told him that maybe things were over for us and that we both needed to live our lives as we were just hurting each other.

I told him that he should go and live out at the dam and put some distance between us until we both knew what we wanted. He was so angry with me. I will never forget his words to me that day, the hatred in his eyes, as if I had just dealt the final blow. He wished the worst on me and told me that he would take everything away from me, including the children.

I told him that we just needed time, that I needed time, and that he should just let things be for a while.

He left the house with so much anger. The boys and I just sat there and cried, not knowing how to deal with his emotions and when we would ever see him again. I tried to phone him, but he refused to speak to me. While I was on the phone trying to reach him later that night, the paramedic arrived at the gate with the news that he had died in a terrible car accident. I was shocked and stunned and actually did not believe the words I was hearing. It was so surreal. I could not even cry. It was as if this was all a big mistake and that I was about to wake up from a very bad dream.

When you arrived, my world fell apart even more as you hit me and screamed at me, pulling my hair and spitting on me, blaming me for what happened. I felt desperate and disillusioned, and a part of me felt responsible for everything.

For weeks after his death, I could not eat or sleep. I was trying to be strong for the boys and for everyone else, but inside I was falling apart. I kept replaying events over and over in my mind: what if I had done this and what if I had done that? I felt as if the world had shut me off and that I didn't deserve to be in it. I thought I was going to lose everything.

I have changed my life and tried to keep things together for the boys, moving house, moving their school, trying to be mom and dad and probably doing a lousy job at it.

Today, I sat and cried for so long that I thought the tears would never dry up. I want to be at peace, now more than ever and feel that I can move on with my life without all the guilt that I have carried with me for so long, without feeling afraid that you might see me again and hate me for trying to move on.

As I write this, I am sitting on a blanket next to a beautiful river. There is so much sadness in my heart. I want you to know how sorry I am that things turned out the way they did. I want you to know that I did not give up on Gareth but that he had given up on life. I did everything I could to be a good wife to him. Maybe I should have done more, but at the time, I was drained and unhappy, and I felt completely helpless.

What happened that night will live with me forever. I wish that Gareth had the strength to reach out to me and his family to help him. Gareth never wanted to die like that – he still had so much to live for. I just don't think he ever saw that.

I watch his beautiful children grow up and wish that he could be here to see them. I am so proud of them, after everything they have been through, how they both still love and idolise him, and I wish that he could be here today to witness their achievements and share in their hopes and dreams. They both miss him so much.

All I ever wanted was for Gareth to be happy, but in my heart, I knew that he needed more from me than I could ever possibly give him. I did not want to see him go the way he did, and I wish that God could have sent down an angel to protect him on the road that night.

I am hoping that this letter might bring about some peace – that you will find it in your hearts to forgive me for what happened. I believe in my heart that Gareth is at peace, and I want you to believe it, too.

I am not asking for a relationship with you. In fact, I think we all know that we need to move on without *each other. We were a big part of each other's lives for a very long time, but I would like to ask you to give me the space I need to move on.*

I cannot even begin to imagine how you have dealt with all of this. There can be no greater loss than that of your own child, especially in the tragic way that Gareth was taken from you.

I am so sorry. So very sorry for the pain and the loss you have suffered. I pray with all my heart and all my soul that you will find peace. That you will be able to put this tragedy behind you and remember Gareth for the gentle giant that he was.

Your daughter-in-law,

Claudia

Claudia carefully folded the letter and placed it inside an envelope. She wrote their name and address on the front. She wondered how they would react when they received it. Would they tear it up into a million little pieces, or would they take the time to read it for what it was worth? She could only hope that it would be the latter. She so desperately wanted to receive their forgiveness. She yearned to be released from the shackles of guilt and blame that they had forced her to wear for all these years. The coldness gnawed at her ankles and cut into her skin. She could hear the scraping of the chain as she dragged it behind her.

Claudia thought about Gareth with so much sadness. She knew that she would always carry a piece of him with her – he had, after all, been a huge part of her life for fifteen years, and it would be impossible for her to simply erase him from her timeline. She thought back fondly to the times that they had laughed together and cried together. She thought about the mountains they had climbed together and the children they had raised together.

Just as quickly as Gareth had entered her life, he had disappeared from it, literally falling out of the visible world and vanishing. There had been no time for goodbyes. There had been no time for apologies. All that was left behind was an empty chair at an empty table – a lifetime of memories that could no longer be matched to a living, breathing soul.

She thought about the emotions, the anger, the fear and the hopelessness; everything that Gareth had endured in the hours before his untimely death, and then her role in it.

She thought about Gareth's family and their shattered lives, and she prayed that they would find peace one day.

But does one ever find peace when a child is wrenched from your life?

Perhaps, like a vehicle on autopilot, one simply carries on.

CHAPTER 23

Seven years later

Sometimes, the heart needs more time to accept what the mind already knows.

It was still dark outside. The moonlight pierced its way through the clouds, fighting against the approaching morning light.

Claudia checked the time. It was four in the morning.

Alex's mobile phone had been vibrating with alerts for most of the evening, and Claudia had slept restlessly, wondering who could be trying to reach him so late into the night.

Their relationship was a far cry from the perfect bond they had forged all those years before. Now, he loved her from a distance. The closeness had a sell-by date. He had become emotionally detached over the years, and Claudia could feel their once-perfect world crumbling beneath her feet.

They had reached a fork in the road, and she could feel her fingers slipping from his grasp as he took his path, and she took hers. She was holding on with everything she had, but he was not looking over his shoulder as she tripped and stumbled behind him in his shadow.

This was not the fairy tale she had imagined.

Alex had woken early to head off to the gym.

All Claudia could think about was his phone.

She pretended she was sleeping.

He left the house, slowly sliding the glass doors behind him.

Claudia crept out of bed. Uneasiness coursed through her veins. She scanned his bedside table. His phone was gone. He had taken it with him.

"Damn it," she thought, pacing the house restlessly, eventually returning to bed.

She tossed and turned for another hour until he returned.

She heard the shower running and realised that he was home.

Knowing that she had a few minutes before he finished, she walked to the lounge. His mobile phone lay innocently on the dining room table.

She held her breath and picked it up, tapping the Home button.

A message.

"*XXX*," it read.

Claudia gasped, feeling her blood run cold. She needed to see more. It was going to hurt like hell, but there was no turning back now.

They had always shared the same passwords. She typed the familiar code into his phone.

"Incorrect Password", it read.

She tried again.

"Incorrect password."

"Shit," she thought. The water was still running in the shower. She felt suspended in time.

She tried another combination.

"Incorrect password"

She typed the original password backwards.

She was in.

And there it was – her worst fears realised.

"*I can't wait to see your breasts,*" it read.

Claudia felt her hands shaking.

"*Only four more hours to go,*" was her reply.

"*I cannot wait,*" he replied.

"*XXX,*" she had replied.

The date stamp read 4:10 am. He must have left the house with *her* in his heart, Claudia thought. And *she* had been awake too, expecting his message. Claudia could feel the life draining out of her body.

She wanted to vomit. She tried to scream, but nothing came out. Her head was spinning.

Her life was flashing past her eyes in slow motion. Gareth. The accident. Alex. Their meeting in the forest. The first time they made love. The life they had built together. The children. Everything she had held on to was going up in flames. Disbelief flooded her body. This couldn't be happening.

"Oh God, please wake me up. This cannot be real," she said to herself over and over again.

She walked into the bedroom, swallowing the bile that was rising in her throat.

"You bastard," she thought. "You fucking bastard."

"Alex," she said, her voice shaking, "could you come out here for a moment?"

She gritted her teeth and swallowed again. He had stepped out of the shower and was wrapping a towel around his waist.

"What's wrong?" he asked, trying to decode the look on her face.

Claudia held his phone out towards him. "Please explain this?"

"Explain what?"

Like a volcano on the brink of erupting, she walked towards him and pushed the phone towards him.

"This," she said. "This message. What the fuck is going on here, Alex?"

She watched the blood drain from his face as he looked down at the screen.

"I don't understand," he said. "What is the problem?"

"*What is the problem?*" Claudia repeated, her voice rising. She felt as if she was trapped in somebody else's nightmare.

"You bloody bastard, Alex," she screamed, the demon that had possessed her now completely in control. "I thought you loved me!"

"I do love you, Claudia," he said defensively. "I love you very much."

"Then what the fuck is going on here?" she screamed. "What have you done?"

"Claudia, it's not what you think," he pleaded with her. "I promise you, it's not what you think!"

"Fuck you, Alex," she said, the tears pouring down her face. "You have ruined everything. Everything I believed in. Everything I've held on to. I thought you were the one!"

For seven years, she had made excuses for Alex's increasing disinterest. It was as if all those years of abuse and hurt and betrayal had shut down his heart and that deep down, he was terrified of opening his soul to Claudia completely. He was always so afraid of being hurt. He had painted her with the same brush that he had painted Christine. "People change when they get married," he had always told her, knowing how much she wanted to marry him. She wanted nothing more than to be his wife. To feel as if, this time, *she* had been worth it. That everything she had endured had not been in vain. To experience the ultimate proof of his love for her. But 'The Future' always had a ring of tentativeness to it. It was hard to explain, but it was certainly felt. The slight hesitation in holding hands. The talk around "his future" rather than "their future".

Claudia could never understand his words.

"Don't you trust me?" she would often ask when the subject of marriage reared its head.

"Of course I trust you, Claudia. I'm just scared. It's not you. It's me."

She never imagined that it was Alex who would be the untrustworthy one.

"Please, Claudia," he begged, losing his grip on her arm as she pulled away from him. "Can we sit down and talk about this?"

"There's nothing to talk about," she sobbed. "It's over. It's done. We're finished. Go to her. She can have you."

Her heart was breaking, and her life was crumbling before her eyes.

"Go and wreck somebody else's life. You have shattered everything I have ever held dear. I have never stopped loving you. I only ever wanted you. I have never betrayed you! Gareth died so that we could be together, and this is what you do? This is how you repay me?"

"Claudia, you've read this all wrong," he pleaded. "You're the only one for me. Nothing has been wasted. I still love you so much!"

Claudia hurriedly dressed and put on her make-up, cursing the mascara as it streaked down her face. Where would she go? Would she even make it through the day? She wanted to die. She wanted the world to swallow her up and suck her into its spinning vortex until she exploded into a million little pieces. She did not think that she would ever be whole again. The rug had been ripped out from under her, and she was falling fast.

And she had no wings to break her fall this time.

There was no Alex to save her.

Her life had come full circle. How wrong she had been. There is no such thing as true love, she thought sadly. She had naively deceived herself into believing that she had stumbled across the Akbar Shah of diamonds, raw and unpolished, while at the same time fragile enough to be shattered into thousands of shards with one careless slip of the hammer.

Claudia thought back to her days at university, her English lecturer pounding out the words to Shakespeare's Macbeth,

Life's but a walking shadow, a poor player

That struts and frets his hour upon the stage

And then is heard no more. It is a tale

Told by an idiot, full of sound and fury

Signifying nothing.

The performance is over. The curtains are drawn, the lights are dimmed, and the players are transformed into new characters with different lines and new beginnings... and the show will always go on.

And so, dear reader, this is how the story ends.

We leave a light on at night so that those we love can find their way home, but there may come a time when we wake in the dimly lit hours of the early morning and find that the light is still burning, and we realise that they are never coming home.

And so, with a heavy heart, we flick the switch and plunge ourselves back into darkness. We close our eyes and hope that one day, perhaps one day, there will be somebody holding a torch for *us*, to light *our* path, so that we too can find our way home.

Epilogue

When we open the book that will become the story of our life, the pages lay naked, wanting, beckoning us, coaxing us, until the words begin to appear, slowly, one by one, where we can clearly make out each letter as its ink blots the page. And then suddenly, in quick succession, sentences and paragraphs and chapters begin to form. Beginnings and endings. Endings and beginnings.

Life holds no promises. There are no five-year guarantees. When life knocks us down, we can choose to fall down the tunnel, spinning and spiralling out of control until finally, we think we have hit rock bottom, only to have another cavern open up and swallow us in deeper. Or we can dust ourselves off, pick ourselves up, straighten our collars, and put that shoe that flew across the room back on. And we can give ourselves a hearty pat on the back and say, "Well done you! You made it! You might be tattered, and your edges might be frayed, and like the Velveteen Rabbit, your insides may be falling out, and the threads holding your eyes in might be somewhat loose, but hey, you're still here."

And do you know what that means? It means that you've still got work to do. The world needs you. Because each day you wake up and go into the world, you have the opportunity to change someone's life.

We are living in the Age of Enlightenment, which means that we are waking up. Sometimes, it is in the act of awakening that we experience the most pain. But it's all good because that pain is moulding us into the greatest version of ourselves, and often, that pain – as raw as it is – can be channelled as a healing tool towards someone else who is drowning in that abyss.

Blame, guilt and retribution are tools of the coward. We cannot change the past. We cannot feed ourselves a daily breakfast of what-ifs and if-onlys. We can only thank the past for its lessons and somehow find peace as we learn to live with the consequences of our choices, knowing that others are living with them, too.

Had the map of her life been offered to Claudia on a silver platter when she entered this world and had the lessons been *hidden* from her, she would have brushed the platter aside and sent it crashing to the floor. Had she *seen* the lessons, the gifts that were going to be revealed to her (admittedly through many hours of alternating screaming and sobbing and desperation), she would have graciously accepted the journey that lay ahead of her.

In hindsight, however, it was probably better that she didn't know.

Disbelief, anger, hurt, betrayal; there was not one of these words that she did not experience in its full magnitude during this decade of her life. She was crushed with the weight of eight years of expectation. *Her* fault, she realised, but the trajectory of that particular course of her life had already determined itself, and she found herself backed up against a wall, just waiting to die. Which she wanted to do. Many times. A bridge over a highway. A dark street where nobody would know. A truck driving the other way. That packet of pills. But somewhere deep in her soul, Claudia knew that giving up was not an option. Life could – and would – still go on, except that this time, she would be writing the terms and conditions.

And so she picked up the shattered pieces. She said her goodbyes. She packed up her belongings. And she left.

Kyle and Ross hugged her and cried with her and told her, with unwavering hope in their eyes, that everything would be okay, as long as they were together. That everything would be okay in the end. Because if it's not okay, it's not the end.

But when nobody was looking or asking, in truth, Claudia felt as if she were dying. The guilt over Gareth's death, compounded with Alex's betrayal, was suffocating her. She sobbed her heart out driving to the office. She sobbed it out driving back home again. She would lie awake at night wondering when that big hole was going to open up. She wondered how long she could keep things up. She wondered whether she could keep her sanity in check. How Claudia wished that her mind would just wander off and never return.

But it stayed.

Because she still had work to do.

As Claudia closed the chapter on that part of her life, her eyes were not dry, and her heart still ached for all that was lost – but her soul was on fire. It was alive for the first time in years. She felt as if she had taken a flaming sword and cut through everything that was holding her back from being the authentic human being that her soul had been crying out for her to be all along.

Claudia learned that sometimes, a person needs to lose everything to find themselves again. Her journey had been the most heart-wrenching rollercoaster ride ever, but, in the end, that's life; sometimes it's great, sometimes it's good, and sometimes it's just downright terrible. But what counts the most, Claudia realised, is that no matter what part of the rollercoaster a person is on, it's the people who are sitting beside you and in front of you and behind you, all screaming, or crying, or laughing with you. And some of them are holding your hand. Or wiping the tears from your eyes. Or kissing your forehead. Or grabbing you by the shoulders and shaking you to wake up.

Alex and Claudia found their way back to each other eighteen months later. They understood their soulmate contract for everything that it was, and they knew that their relationship was over – forever. Alex, as soulmates often do, had come into her life to shake it up, to shake *her* up, and to force her to open her eyes to everything that she had been missing. She had, ironically, been there to do the same for him.

It took her some time, but eventually, she made peace with herself – and with Alex. She forgave him for his meanderings when it became apparent that all was not as it had appeared to be. He had been a complete asshole – there was no questioning that – but, like Claudia, he was still figuring himself out. She had been his channel. Their ending, as seemingly ill-timed as it had presented itself, was a *necessary* ending.

Kyle and Ross grew into fine young men. Although their journey was difficult, it gave them a greater sense of empathy and connectedness towards other human beings.

Claudia learned to love herself again. When she was ready, she opened the door and welcomed love back in, and her heart began to mend.

She still speaks to Gareth when nobody is watching.

Acknowledgements

To my precious children, Brandon and Justin, I love you with every fibre of my being, and I am so incredibly sorry that my choices took your father away from you. He has never stopped loving you, and I promise you that he walks beside you every day.

To Grant's family, the souls who were destroyed when your son and brother left this earth so suddenly, leaving you with more questions than answers, I will forever carry the pain of your loss. Please know that I never wanted Grant's journey here to end the way it did. For that, I am deeply sorry.

To each and every soul who has travelled with me on my perilous journey of bringing my story into the light, I thank you with all the gratitude in my heart. The list is too long to fit on this page, but I know that you know who you are and the role you have played during my voyage towards self-liberation and inner peace.

A special word of thanks to Lisa Botha – thank you for your pragmatism, your unfaltering support, and your love, right up until the very end.

To Chris Ferreira – thank you for helping me to keep it together through my darkest hours and for your unwavering compassion, empathy and care.

To my parents, Denny and Mo, my sister Kate, and my brother Magnus – I will always be thankful to you for grounding me, for never questioning me, and for always standing by my choices.

To the Fire Claw Tribe – without the accountability that this special group has brought with it, this book would not have seen its completion so quickly.

To Donna McCallum and Nick Hawke for inspiring me to start the writing process. To Justin Cohen for inspiring me to complete it.

And finally, to Ceri James – thank you for being my greatest teacher.

About the Author

Phillipa Mitchell was born to British parents in South Africa in December 1972.

Besides being an author, she is an accomplished writer, ghostwriter, editor and entrepreneur and has worked in the bookselling and publishing industry since the early nineties. Her passion as a writer and ghostwriter is working on non-fiction material, especially memoirs, biographies, business books and inspirational books.

She has raised two fine young men who are her pride and joy and, thanks to their good genes, are both exceptionally talented in the creative arts.

PHILLIPA MITCHELL

She is a child of Africa and is passionate about its people, its culture and its magic.

Four in the Morning is her first published work.

www.ingramcontent.com/pod-product-compliance
Lightning Source LLC
Chambersburg PA
CBHW022024290426
44109CB00014B/737